To all those with big side-hustle ideas and dreams – let's make them a reality.

CONTENTS

INTRODUCTION

We've all had that moment in the shower, on the train or while on a run, when an idea pops into our head, that eureka moment. You tell yourself this is the next groundbreaking idea that the world hasn't seen. You linger over it, you sleep on it, then you tell your friends about it – or maybe you don't? And, well, it never comes alive. That dream doesn't become a reality. Most of the time it's not that you don't believe in the idea, but it's the barriers that get in the way – such as lack of self-belief, not being sure about where to start, or even thinking you don't possibly have the time.

Often the idea is so grand that it scares you, but you just need to start small and take it one step at a time. Take small actions on a daily basis, and over time these will accumulate into the grand vision that you have for your side-hustle idea. You'll see from several examples in this book that everything starts small, and the most important thing is that in order to get ahead you just need to start. Start where you are, with what you know and what you have – that's the gift of this book.

I wrote *Side Hustle in Progress* for women who have always spoken about starting a business but have never actually got around to doing so. This is a practical guide with a framework that I and many other women have used to kickstart an idea. What has made it work for us? We're all just like you, everyday women with an idea and the audacity to say, 'I'll try'; while some even said, 'I'm not just going to try but I'm going to absolutely smash it!' Are you ready to join us?

Beyond helping you to find the self-belief you need to get started, *Side Hustle in Progress* will show you how to validate your ideas, how to get people talking about your side hustle and how to get yourself into publications where you can get more eyes on your business. Every experience in life has a lesson and you'll learn a few from myself, the inspirational female founders that I've interviewed, and many others through your own personal journey of side hustling.

Before we dive deep, let me clear up what my own definition of side hustling is. Simply put, it's anything that you do outside your main full-time employment. However, side hustles carry a more entrepreneurial connotation than merely taking on a second job like delivering newspapers at the weekend or stacking the shelves at your local grocery store.

Starting a side hustle has become an extremely popular choice; it's a thing of pride to call yourself a founder and to be doing something entrepreneurial. It's trendy. Entrepreneurship looks sexy and glamorous, but it's not always easy and it's certainly not a quick way to make money. However, it can be a great way to monetise your passion project or provide an extra stream of income – apparently you need several of these to become a millionaire.

We are a lucky generation as we have the power of the internet to help us launch a business in literally seconds, whether it's a marketplace on sites like like eBay, or starting an e-commerce brand on Squarespace, or even just launching it on Instagram. Access to social media means we have direct and immediate access to our potential customers while giving us a global presence. But don't be fooled, there is no such thing as an overnight success and you'll still need to put in the work – the *right* work.

In 2018, the *Independent* reported that almost 40 per cent of UK workers have a side hustle and this number is expected to increase to half of the adult population by 2030. These side hustlers generated a massive £72 billion for the UK economy in 2017, which shows how important entrepreneurs are to the economy.

Fast forward to COVID-19, and as of July 2020, 85,000 businesses have launched online or joined online marketplaces, four months after the pandemic began, with the fashion and apparel sector leading the way (someone say loungewear!). Despite the world now going through the challenging transition of coming out of the pandemic, there are still opportunities to launch a business. In the US, businesses are growing at the fastest rate since 2007. Why? A mix of necessity and opportunities, as reported by the *Wall Street Journal*. But in this same article, it was also reported that 'The US lost more businesses during the first three months of the crisis than it normally does in an entire year.' As some were sadly shutting shop, new ones were being birthed.

THE ALISON ROSE REVIEW OF FEMALE ENTREPRENEURSHIP

An independent review of female entrepreneurship commissioned by the Treasury – The Alison Rose Review of Female

Entrepreneurship – found that only 6 per cent of women in the UK run their own businesses, compared to 15 per cent of women in Canada, almost 11 per cent of women in the US, and over 9 per cent of women in Australia and the Netherlands. The key to improving the UK stats will be to ensure that women have access to the advice and support they need to fully develop their entrepreneurial skills.

This is why I started For Working Ladies in 2016, a platform to support women like you – women who are looking to start a side hustle – but ultimately a platform with the mission to advance women and girls, professionally and personally; because the two certainly cannot be divided. I've also just recently been working on another business with a similar mission, leicour.com, which is focused on women in full-time employment, and women who have often been overlooked for leadership roles and lack the support and community they need.

Now back to those stats. The number of female entrepreneurs in the UK is incredibly low despite the fact that more and more women want to own a business. The underlying factors are fear and a perceived belief that they are not supposed to be business owners. These are things that I will address right at the beginning of this book, because how you feel determines the actions you take and it's important we get our mindsets in the right place.

Side Hustle in Progress is by no means an attempt to look down on having a day job or disregard the corporate experience – I don't believe in pushing this narrative because at the end of the day entrepreneurs have to hire people too! Having women in leadership roles in corporate organisations is just as important as having more female-founded and owned businesses. Both have equal merit, but here we will address the latter.

My side hustle has changed my life and yours can do the same for you, too. Whether it's a product, an e-commerce business or even a podcast, ideas change lives.

HOW THIS BOOK WILL WORK

When writing *Side Hustle in Progress,* I thought about the full lifecycle of becoming a founder of a side hustle. This book covers what I wish I knew before starting, the type of person I needed to be and the important things that are often missed.

I have divided the book into five parts: Before the Journey, Taking Off, Branding Your Idea, The Important Stuff and Life After Side Hustling. Each part is an explanation of the different phases you will go through in starting your side hustle. Within each part are different chapters followed by exercises to get you thinking and taking action, and also interviews with women who run businesses of their own – some are small, while some are large and have even been acquired. Their advice is practical, relatable and insightful and a great way to learn how they made it happen. These interviews were conducted towards the end of 2020 and have been paraphrased by myself.

Side Hustle in Progress is a mixture of my opinion, based on my experience, my research and also advice gleaned from experts and other founders.

1

BEFORE THE JOURNEY

There's nothing like being mentally prepared for the journey ahead, and that is what this first part is all about – from mindset to wellbeing to productivity, we will cover it all.

These topics are usually found at the end of most business books, if they're even included! But I've gone ahead and put them first to demonstrate how important I think they are. I don't subscribe to the belief that running a side hustle or a full-time business needs to be all hustle and grind to the detriment of your health, or that you must hide your femininity in order to succeed. Don't get me wrong, it is hard and some people won't be able to hack it, but if I have learned one thing along the way, it's that if I'm not mentally and physically well, everything else will fail. As the popular saying goes, 'You can't give from an empty well.'

THE ENTREPRENEURIAL MINDSET

'Think right, to show up right.'

Over the years I have been curious to find out what makes the most successful people – not just entrepreneurs but leaders, activists and innovators. Because as far as I'm concerned, having the audacity to start something is a big deal. Some say it's talent, others say it's grit. This curiosity motivated me to start my podcast 'How I Made it Happen', where I tend to ask guests, 'What made you think it would work? What gave you the audacity to start?' It also led me to dig deep into research books such as *Grit: The Power of Passion and Perseverance*, by Angela Duckworth, to understand what actually brings about success.

After interviewing hundreds of successful entrepreneurs, I've realised they all have something in common – even the ones that 'fail' the first couple of times – and that is a way of thinking, a mindset, and a few similar characteristics.

Why a whole chapter on mindset? Because it has been proven that the way we think determines how we deal with situations and setbacks, how we show up in life and how we develop ourselves.

What we've been taught is that those who succeed are the people who are extremely talented, incredibly smart (with high IQs) and have always excelled in life. Some of you may feel that none of the above applies to you, which might make you think this will limit what you can achieve. You'll learn from this book that you don't have to know everything about the industry you are going into, nor do you need to be super talented to succeed, but you do need to have the attitude of never giving up, of being willing to learn, fail and start again. That is what sets people up for success.

Investors usually like backing second-time founders because they can see these people understand the road ahead and have probably learned lessons from doing it once before. Also, statistically the second attempt succeeds more than the first one. Second-time founders also have access to a bigger network. So don't fear failure, it has its rewards.

You don't have to have attended university, or have any professional qualifications to succeed. Success is not dependent on formal education. Don't get me wrong, formal education is important. However, although my MSc was in International Business, there is absolutely nothing better than hands-on experience.

I've been asked a few times how I've managed to build For Working Ladies alongside a 9–5 job. I put it down to passion for what I'm trying to achieve and a way of thinking – being open to learning things I don't know and asking questions of those who can help. I'm also always willing to make things work, and not fazed by getting it wrong and starting again. Writing

Side Hustle in Progress has been a new challenge; I've never written a book before, but here I am with my début, trusting myself that I'll learn from my own lessons, which has been challenging and also frightening.

The greatest reward you receive from launching an idea is not necessarily the return of profits or having a successful business, but the person you become and the mindset you cultivate in the process. It is the best form of self-development. This is invaluable; it shows that you have the ability to dream and fearlessly go after whatever it is that you desire. The brilliant thing about this type of mindset is that it can be learned. Mindsets can also be changed, because the mind is like a muscle, but it won't change overnight. Those mind shifts come with time, lessons and experiences. This right here is more valuable than any business strategy that you'll learn.

Read on for a list of qualities that are important in developing your entrepreneurial mindset and achieving outstanding success.

SELF-BELIEF

There is absolutely no point in embarking on the journey of starting a side hustle if you feel you are incapable of doing it. You may as well not bother starting. That limiting self-belief that you have created about yourself will be your experience, but it doesn't have to be that way. Our belief in ourselves guides how we show up in the world, it determines whether we become the person we want to be and whether we accomplish the goals we set for ourselves.

> The beginning of failure is the lack of self-belief,
> and the beginning of success is an abundance of
> self-belief.

In his book *The Magic of Thinking Big*, Professor David J. Schwartz writes, 'Belief, the "I'm-positive-I-can" attitude, generates the power, skill and energy needed to do. When you believe I-can-do-it, the how-to-do-it develops.'

It's a straightforward formula: Believe – Feel – Do.

It is not wishful thinking, which only requires you to dream. You can't wish a six-figure side hustle, but you can believe you are capable of creating one, then start to observe and learn what it takes to create this. Then, of course, finally you can take action. Can you see the difference? Self-belief must be coupled with action.

Your self-belief is what gives people confidence in you. Have the audacity to believe in yourself. You can achieve great things.

How to develop self-belief

- Feed your mind with stories of self-belief. Start with listening to a few of the podcasts I have listed in the resources section, read about stories of those who have brought their ideas alive, not just the successes but the failures too. As you are listening and watching, take notes so you can refer back to their learnings.

- What are your limiting self-beliefs? Write them down and for each one create a mantra to counter it. Make time in your day for when you can speak this into existence. I suggest doing it in the morning, when you rise.
- With each limiting belief you have listed, write down the action you can take to conquer it. For example, if your limiting belief is 'I can never succeed at selling products online because I do not understand social media,' the action you take to conquer this is to educate yourself on social media. This could be through reading books, watching YouTube videos or even taking a course. There is definitely a solution to every limiting self-belief.
- Create a vision of what you want to achieve. You can do this by making a vision board or even just writing down a paragraph of what you want to achieve in the future. I have a personalised diary titled 'Liz's Manifestation Journal', and in here are my BIG future ideas of everything, not just business. Take the desires within you, get them down on paper and take action.
- Surround yourself with people who believe in you. Make a list of those who make you feel capable and spend more time with them. Our circle has the power to influence us and you don't need bad energy. Make sure you evaluate the advice of others and ask yourself if some people are worthy of being in your space. I create absolutely no room for anyone that wants to plant seeds of doubt within me, but I do make sure I take critical feedback and filter through

what needs to be taken onboard and what needs to be
trashed.

- Focus on your strengths. Create a list of what you know
  your strengths to be and also ask friends and colleagues to
  name the first five that come to mind – refer to this list
  often so you are reminded of your magic!

CURIOSITY

Have the mind of a child, forever curious and with a hunger for
novelty. As we grow older we tend to lose our sense of discovery as we have less time on our hands and want to avoid risk
and inefficiency.

I explored many options with For Working Ladies; I was
always open to opportunities of trying a new business concept.
Back in 2016, it started out as a media company and I began
to realise that it would require huge amounts of funds in order
to maintain and grow. I managed 20 writers on my own; what
did I know about being an Editor in Chief? But I did it. I eventually burned out, though, so I decided to try a simpler business model. I always made sure to understand why things
didn't work and research the alternative solutions I had – that
was my curiosity in action.

The people who have gone on to create unique ideas are
those who have continued to be curious, have given themselves room to explore and seek more than what is on the
surface by asking why and rethinking the normal way of doing
things. Take Airbnb, for example: who would have ever thought
we would be renting out our homes to complete strangers?

People thought it was completely crazy, but curiosity led them to discover how it could work. In the first couple of years when the founders were only making $200 a week, they decided to use the money to fly out to New York to meet their customers and ask them questions. In doing so, they discovered that the main problem customers faced was that the pictures of most listings weren't good. So they bought a camera and went door-to-door to take better pictures.

Curiosity meant continuing to understand the needs of the customers by asking questions, understanding behaviours and wondering why they took certain actions and not others. There's also Butternut Box, a sort of Deliveroo for dogs, which was started by two ex-investment bankers and provides freshly prepared dog food. Who would have thought that dogs would ever get such a treat? Curiosity led the founders to understand why their own dogs were getting sick from processed packaged food and so they decided to feed them home-cooked food. When their dogs felt better they discovered there was a gap in the market and ran with the idea. Curiosity allows you the opportunity to think outside the box.

Be aware that curiosity can also annoy people; they may want to move forward with the bare minimum of information while you desire to dig deeper and question the status quo. Curiosity will always bring about the best solutions for problems.

How to develop curiosity

- Read widely, beyond your area of interest.
- Explore new things: visit restaurants you wouldn't usually try, watch documentaries, travel and experience new

cultures, even if it is local – you'd be surprised how a bus out of your neighbourhood will allow you to discover something new.

- Be willing to ask the questions that no one is asking, the foolish ones. Dig deeper and discover more than what is on the surface. Curiosity is a muscle and will need to be exercised.
- Rethink the usual way of doing things, which means always saying no to the usual approach and discovering a new one.

RESILIENCE

When I think of resilience, I imagine an elastic band that is stretched to its limits, then once released it snaps back together. Resilience is having the ability to snap back in the event of any challenges, problems and setbacks that you experience in life, but not just snap back, come back stronger. Bringing an idea to life will stretch you and you'll experience challenges that you have not before, but having the ability to know how to cope better and recover more quickly will be a superpower that you'll need.

The most resilient people are not superhuman, because like most traits these things are learned and mastered through drawing upon past experiences, whether they are life-changing or not.

How to develop resilience

- Each time you experience being resilient or getting over something difficult, journal about the moment. That way you build a bank of experiences that you can draw upon when you're struggling.

- Create affirmations about the above experiences to help you remember them in times of overwhelm.
- Become more self-aware – take an inventory of yourself and your skills, gather data and understand how you could better manage challenges and adversity. Knowing this will help you move through the experience quicker with time.
- Reframe the narrative, change how you view negative situations. Pay very close attention to the words you use when situations arise and the way you talk to yourself. See challenges as catalysts for growth and learning.

COURAGEOUSLY CONQUERING FEAR

'Courage is resistance to fear, mastery of fear,
not absence of fear.'
Mark Twain

Before confidence comes courage – you need courage to conquer fear, courage to try to do new things. According to Ward Andrews, CEO of Drawbackwards, 'Fear is a primal human emotion, it's what our brains default to.' To rewire our brain's default state, we must continue to conquer the fear by applying courage. Even when you have conquered the fear it never completely disappears, but as Ward shares, 'that doesn't mean you have to give it control or allow it to drive'. The more we face uncomfortable experiences, the more courageous we become.

I wish I could tell you that you will feel no ounce of fear when it comes to putting your idea out into the world, but I'd be lying to you. You will on several occasions question yourself, ask if what you are doing is going to work, mostly out of fear. That's completely fine, because you must always view a business idea as an experiment. This is a learning curve and you will continue to refine your idea as you go along.

If we go back to the Alison Rose Review of Female Entrepreneurship mentioned in my introduction, one of the findings showed that women were held back from starting a business because of fear. Fear keeps you in a box. Fear holds you back from progressing. Allowing the false scenarios that do not exist to play around in our heads is not action – we must take practical steps to do something to conquer and defeat this fear.

So, what do those practical steps look like for you?

How to develop the courage to conquer fear

- Acknowledge that fear is a real emotion and everyone feels it every now and again. Embrace it, don't run from it, own it and know that you are in control.
- Winston Churchill said, 'Fear is a reaction. Courage is a decision.' Decide to act in courage despite the fear. Make decisions by taking action that moves you a step forward. For instance, buying this book is taking action. Sharing your idea with people is taking action. Doing research is taking action. Continue to take action and that will allow you to continually build courage.

- Bet on yourself; despite the fear, believe that you are capable.
- Be comfortable with failing. The moment you can get comfortable with this, it will allow you to take more steps that conquer fear.

HAVE A GROWTH MINDSET VS FIXED MINDSET

Dr Caroline Dweck, Stanford University psychologist and author of *Mindset: The New Psychology of Success*, believes there are two main mindsets with which we can navigate life: growth and fixed. She coined these two terms to describe the underlying beliefs that people have about learning and intelligence.

A 'growth mindset' insists that you are capable of learning, growing and exploring new concepts, and stretching your existing abilities through your efforts, your strategies and with help from others. This mindset thrives on challenges and does not see failure as failing but as learning. Carol Dweck believes that this is the mindset that allows people to be successful during the most challenging times in their lives.

However, a 'fixed mindset' assumes that you are only given a certain amount of intelligence, character and ability, which is ultimately set in stone. A fixed mindset does not believe in putting in effort or getting help. Your failure defines who you are and there will be no improvement.

To put this into perspective, here is an example: a young lady wants to start a skincare brand that requires an understanding of cosmetic science. A fixed mindset says, 'I won't be able to learn cosmetic science, I was crap at science in school. I won't bother with that idea.' The growth mindset says, 'I wasn't good at science in school but I can try out this cosmetic science course and see how it goes. There's a way to bring this skincare brand alive.'

You don't need to know everything, but you must be open to learning and growing – this is an important pillar for every successful entrepreneur, because in the beginning they become the jack of all trades. They're not naturally born like that, but they learn to do it – especially when they have no budget to hire the 'experts'! There will surely be an opportunity to outsource, but when the opportunity isn't there, you must learn to flex your growth muscles and get things done. This, to me, is the real entrepreneurial mindset. A growth mindset is something that you can nurture and develop, it just takes a little recalibrating of your mindset to a more positive, forward-thinking one.

How to develop a growth mindset

- Be open to learning new and complex things. When things seem hard, challenge yourself to get to grips with them.
- Frame failure as an opportunity to develop. You will get some things wrong, which is brilliant as that is an opportunity to learn from them and develop yourself.
- Approach issues with a problem-solving mindset.

OWNING YOUR FEMININITY

In the early days of starting out in my career, I had applied for a recruitment managerial role in the finance sector. The interviewer told me that I'd be more suited for the hospitality sector as I'm 'soft'. That piece of feedback from that moment changed how I showed up at work. I was intentionally more 'aggressive' and felt that my 'soft' nature wouldn't get me far. I've since come to learn that I made a huge mistake taking on that feedback and have decided to lean into my femininity as it's my superpower. Most of the attitudes and sentiments in the entrepreneurial space are very masculine: there is an implicit assumption that men are, by default, what a business founder looks and acts like. How they approach business is how we should all approach business and how they act is the 'right' way to act. Because of this, you may feel the need to change in order to get ahead. Don't; instead, own who you are and don't feel like you have to fit the mould of what the world thinks a business leader looks like.

*

Most of these characteristics are interlinked and rarely ever show up in silos. So as you begin to develop one, you'll realise the others will naturally show up.

This is just the start of the journey; although the entrepreneurial mindset is important, you'll still need killer branding,

PR, a deep understanding of your product/service, and much more – all of which I'll touch on in the next couple of chapters.

GET TO WORK

1. Journal the times you experienced resilience and what you learned.
2. Create a mantra that you can add to your morning routine; think of where you are most struggling and reframe the situation with the mantra. Change this regularly, maybe weekly or monthly.
3. Who are the individuals that you feel have an entrepreneurial mindset? Who could you learn from? Do they have interviews online? Podcasts? Videos? Do you have direct access to them, could you consider sending them an email and asking for specific advice?
4. Make a list of things that you fear the most about starting a side hustle, reframe your mindset and write next to each fear what you can do to overcome it.

VICTORIA PREW

CEO and Co-founder of HURR Collective

WHO IS VICTORIA PREW?

Victoria Prew is a former chartered surveyor who left the corporate world to start building the UK's first peer-to-peer wardrobe rental platform, HURR Collective, alongside co-founder Matthew Geleta, at the end of 2017. HURR allows women to share their luxury clothes in seconds – by listing your wardrobe items for rent or by browsing and borrowing your favourites. Although Victoria is interested in fashion and admits that the brand is fuelled by fashion, HURR is a tech company, not a fashion company, which is the pillar of its success. The site utilises leading ID-verification software, AI personal styling and extensive peer reviews to ensure customers feel safe and secure.

VICTORIA'S STORY

We came up with the idea of HURR at the end of 2017 because we wanted to position the business in the sharing economy. We had watched the rise of Uber and Airbnb and the fact that they had tapped into a whole generation of people who were not used to renting their homes or their cars and to us the next logical step was wardrobes. The second trend I looked into was the idea of wanting to own less and the massive shift towards sustainability. The more research we did the more compelled we became that we had a business case — we wanted to provide something different.

What I didn't know was if this business would stand in the market, if I could raise funding and it would be scalable? I looked at the number one player in the market and looked at all the models, pros and cons, read research reports, looked at why it was working and the challenges they had in the early days. I then looked at all the companies who had done peer-to-peer rentals and failed, and went through why they did not work – they were a fashion first business and did not understand the importance of tech. Always look at the people doing it well and why the business had failed; and then look wider and beyond, and for us, that was the likes of Airbnb, Uber, etc. It's important not to stay in this narrow mindset; get fresh and new ideas by looking at other companies outside of what you are building.

Our minimal viable product was not glossy. I and my co-founder built this. He focused on the coding and I focused on the UI/UX, which is the technical look and experience of the app — the number one hurdle of building a tech product is the cost of building it, and we saved hundreds of pounds by doing it ourselves. We spent around a year building the platform, with 1–2 months in BETA testing.

I never knew anything about UI/UX but you can learn anything on the internet these days. I took loads of online tutorials and, most importantly, I surrounded myself with people who knew what they were talking about and were experts in this space. I looked at businesses I admired, found their product and UX teams and reached out to ask for help.

I knew we could build the HURR platform, I knew how we wanted things to look and that we could do it. It was just a matter of time and investing in learning. When you're transitioning into things that you're not necessarily good at, the most important thing is, how can you be credible? You learn about it! There was nothing that I didn't know about building a peer-to-peer platform and a marketplace when I launched HURR — this is most probably the most researched project I have done throughout two degrees, a full-time job and professional exams.

Being hands on deck and running a business is different from studying for an MBA or any professional qualification. I wanted to learn by doing, so we did a lot of testing and pivoting. I love to learn new things that I am interested in but it's also good to understand what you are good at. It is very important. HURR would never have existed if I did not have my co-founder to build the app with me.

To be an entrepreneur you have to be able to take risks. For the first time in my life and the history of a lot of businesses, there have been no answers as to how we handle the global pandemic. The best CEOs and mentors do not know how to navigate this but, frankly, we have had to trust our gut and make quick decisions, we have survived and recovered revenue-wise because we were able *to make decisions very quickly as to how we were going to get through this.*

VICTORIA'S WORDS OF WISDOM

- Run before you can walk – anyone can walk but not everyone can run. By the time we launched HURR, we had built an email waiting list of 10,000 interested users and a full community engaged in the product we were launching so we could take off when the product was ready.
- Have an 80 per cent attitude, which means be happy with at least 80 per cent of what you have. If you always strive for perfection you will never launch. Things will always go wrong.
- Think through all the processes, what could go wrong and what you would do if they do.

@victoriaprew
@hurrcollective
hurrcollective.com

DETERMINING YOUR SIDE HUSTLE

'Everything starts with a thought, making a decision and then action.'

The purpose of this book is to help you bring your ideas to life, now and in the future. Whether that idea is small or big or whether you decide to keep it as a side hustle or eventually pursue it full time, start now, because opportunities come and go and ideas wait for no one. Don't you hate it when someone launches a business that you once had an idea for? Start it as a side hustle and get it off the ground. But in order for that to happen you must consider the following things so that you can sustain it alongside your full-time commitment.

I have been running For Working Ladies as a side hustle for the last four years. As I have stepped into more senior roles in my career and received more responsibilities, I have had to decide where to prioritise my time. This has meant I have had to scale back on certain activities with my side hustle, such as the amount of events we run, and do I want to do these monthly or host an annual conference ? Whatever you do, try to determine what your side hustle will look like from early on.

VISION

A life coach once asked me, 'Liz, what type of working life do you want in the future, five years from now?' She asked me to get really clear on it, to visualise the hours I'd be working, what my daily routine would look like and who I'd be working with. Most times, we have control of where we end up in life — whether it is by taking intentional steps or accepting what comes at us. Having a clear vision allows you to understand the steps you need to take now in order to get to your desired future.

What is the end goal for your side hustle? if you can think ahead this will determine how you start and plan. Do you hope for your idea to continue as a side hustle or do you one day want this to be your full-time job? If so, how many months or years do you want this to remain as a side hustle and what do you need to do in order to transition it from your side hustle? Once you start working on your idea this will become clearer, as you'll see the opportunities that could arise.

Identify your skills and areas of interest

The best side hustles are the ones in which you can invest your current skills, as this will allow you to see quick results – even better when you have an interest in that industry. That being said, you can always learn the skills you do not have or outsource to those that do.

Have you got the time?

Determine how much time you have for a side hustle – are you willing to commit weekends only or both weekends and weekday evenings, or do you plan to spend mornings working on it before you head to your full-time commitment? You must evaluate before you get started what time you have for it and what time you are willing to give, then ask if it is enough to allow you to really bring this idea to life. When Emma Gannon wrote her first bestseller (she has five now) she was initially working in a 9-to-5, and she made a request to her line manager to take Wednesday afternoons off so she could work on her book. Likewise, as I am writing my book, I have used two weeks of my annual leave to get started. What are the options you have and what are you willing to give up?

Don't forsake your full-time commitment

I remember a conversation with a friend, in which she said, 'My employer is my investor, they enable my side hustle.' What she meant here was her main source of income was important to her and enabled her to continue to run her side hustle — don't forget this. While you are working your contracted hours, make sure to give that job your full attention and commitment.

Money

Some side hustles may not produce income immediately. For instance, if you need to use a few months for market research and product development, make sure you use that time wisely while also building interest from potential customers. Most side hustles don't cost much to get off the ground, but some will – are you willing to invest money into this idea? If so, how much? You need to be aware of your spend before it happens.

Conflict of interest

If you are starting something that is similar to the company you work for, it is important that you review your contract, employee handbook and anything else you've signed; read all of the fine print and check there isn't any potential conflict of interests. Some companies don't like employees working on side hustles, whereas some appreciate the self-starter attitude. It's important you find out where your company stands with this. While you are there, do not use company resources for your side hustle and do not poach clients or use their intellectual property!

Commitment

Are you ready to commit to something that may not bring you any money in the first couple of months or may require you to give up your evenings? That may mean less time with friends and family and more spent on your idea. And it's not just about time; are you ready to fail, to make mistakes, to feel like sometimes you don't know what you are doing? That feeling may come sometimes but, even though we know that feelings don't equate to the truth, will you stay committed to this? Your commitment determines the success of your side hustle, and lack of it is one of the reasons many fail. Have a candid conversation with yourself about whether or not this is something you're willing to pursue and make sacrifices for. You know best.

Five reasons why you should start a side hustle

1. It allows you to diversify your skill set.
2. A side hustle brings financial security: I once was let go by an organisation that had lost their biggest client and I was given less than a day's notice; I no longer lived at home and I had bills to pay. Luckily I had been working on For Working Ladies on the side, had secured some brand partnerships and had upcoming events, and in under a month I was able to make around £6,000. The beauty of it is that I was also doing work that impacted women in a positive way.
3. Starting a side hustle brings about new opportunities, as many founders have been able to cross over into other things. For example, you may be recognised and asked to join a board, be selected as a judge for an awards ceremony, offered a book deal or even offered a job because of the impact you have delivered.
4. It provides an opportunity to build wealth.
5. You can work with your passions – something you may not be able to do in your full-time employment.

GET TO WORK

1. What is it you want to achieve with a side hustle? What is the long-term goal? In 12 months from now, where would you want it to be? Write down the overall goals, then break these down into quarterly goals and go from there. This will give you clarity on where you are heading and allow you to consider what it will take to get you there.

2. How much time are you willing to dedicate to a side hustle? Look at your current lifestyle and work out the hours and days you can commit. Be honest. There is no wrong or right answer.

3. How much money are you willing to invest? Are you willing to invest your savings?

4. What could potentially hold you back from starting a side hustle and how can you work around this? Think about the biggest obstacles you might face.

5. Is there a conflict of interest with your full-time job? Be sure to check your contract and, if necessary, ask HR to be completely sure!

AFUA OSEI

Co-founder of She Leads Africa and Partnerships Strategist

WHO IS AFUA OSEI?

Afua Osei is a partnerships strategist who helps digital entrepreneurs build the skills, systems and confidence to work with the corporate clients of their dreams.

As a co-founder of She Leads Africa, Afua built a digital lifestyle platform for millennial multicultural women, reaching more than 800,000 women across over 100 countries. In addition to building a thriving community, Afua secured international partnerships with brands like Facebook, Google, Unilever, Nestlé, Samsung, Estée Lauder, Visa and L'Oréal to design culturally relevant and data-driven engagement campaigns. In December 2016, the company rang the Closing Bell at the New York Stock Exchange.

AFUA OSEI'S STORY

Although I ran She Leads Africa full-time, it started out as a side hustle. I had taken part in quite a few programmes in the past and I was missing the energy I got from working on something. I am obsessed with building and wanted to do more impact-driven work, which my consulting job was not giving me the opportunity to do. I decided to set up SLA with a colleague of mine, although the idea actually started when I was at university, but I struggled to get real traction. In 2014 SLA launched with its first event.

My advice for anyone who is thinking about their business model is that it is not enough to think about what you want to get paid for. You've also got to think about how you are going to get paid because the how and the mechanics will really influence what your business model would look like.

We realised in the early days that B2C, which is business to consumers, was not possible for us and we had three months to pull together the first event. So we started looking at corporate organisations and from there we had to think about 'What brand right now needs to position themselves in this market and in this space?' SLA is focused on social impact with women and entrepreneurship, so we knew there were some brands that would want to align with our vision.

My process for securing brand partnerships was quite straightforward. It started with research, with a list of about 10 to 15 potential brands that could align with our visions. From there we started to think about where we had connections, who could help us make introductions — this will always be much better than sending a cold email or adding someone on LinkedIn. We started reaching out to our network and specifically asked for links to decision makers – often the marketing manager or the person heading the corporate communications department.

This was our first event, so when it came to credibility we really had to rely on what our connections would say about us during the introductions. Some could comment on the work we do in our 9-to-5s or other impact projects we had worked on — this helped to build trust and credibility with the organisations we were looking to work with. The brands decided to give us a shot based on the recommendations. We now had to make sure that we actually delivered on the experience that we said we would and being as close to that as possible so we could build a track record that would allow us to go and pitch to someone else. Now we had solved the problem of how we were going to make money as a media and events company.

When it comes to securing these partnerships, make sure you do as much research as possible. Look into what their priorities are – do they have any ongoing crisis management they may need support with? Sometimes it can be the fact that they are not known in the industry you work in; for us it was women in entrepreneurship — we would show them what other organisations are doing in this space and how they too could support the agenda of women in business.

If your business is just getting started with partnerships, one of the key things you should focus on is vision. Speak about how they could plug into the vision and talk about metrics and the impact you can offer – that could be media, lead generation or sales. Lastly, show them what your plan is and how you intend to *roll it out over a set period of time. Let them see you are thinking about it in a structured and logical way.*

One of the pros of the Business to Business (B2B) model is that you are working with bigger budgets and fewer people. *However, the con is, it takes much longer to secure a B2B deal and your revenue could be high or it could be low — it really depends on the client. As a result, we decided going forward we would have a mixed model of B2B and B2C, which means we would be selling to both consumers and businesses. We started offering coaching, masterclasses and membership subscriptions to the women in the community; we tried a range of things and stuck with what the community actually wanted.*

Like most people, I never had the intention to be an entrepreneur. *The opportunity to transition into it full time was when the demand for brands came, when brands in and outside the country were wanting to work with us. This was enough validation that it was time to make it my main business.*

AFUA'S WORDS OF WISDOM

- We all complain about social media algorithms but that shouldn't keep you from connecting to your audience. Regardless of the size of your business or audience, start today with developing a personal and direct way to speak to them. This could be via email, text message or private group. It may take more effort in the short term but it will produce great results in the long run.

- The size of your audience doesn't determine the size of your impact. Most of us won't become celebrities with millions of followers, but that doesn't mean we can't all contribute our skills and talents to impact someone else's life.
- You can quit clients too. If you're working with people who don't respect your work, your boundaries or your expertise, it's absolutely okay to walk away. Do so with kindness and professionalism, but you don't have to feel pressured to work with those that don't align with your values. New opportunities will come that will enable you to stay true to who you are.

@helloafua
@sheleadsafrica
afuaosei.com
www.sheleadsafrica.org

YOUR POWER CIRCLE

*'We aren't self-made, we are the result of
the people we know and work with.'*

I recently came across the book *The Unfair Advantage* by Ash Ali and Hasan Kubba, which provided a fresh and honest perspective on how some entrepreneurs become successful because of their unfair advantages, or what some would deem as privileges. In this instance, an unfair advantage is something that cannot be easily copied and puts you in a better position than others. It's important for all of us to know, develop and leverage our own unfair advantages so we too can succeed in life.

In some cases, that unfair advantage is your network and the strong connections you have created – who you know, who you can turn to for answers on questions that have been echoing in your head, who will make introductions when necessary or who can share your side hustle with their engaged large following. That is an unfair advantage, especially when it comes to running a side hustle. It's also one you can create for yourself, one you should continue to develop and leverage.

In an article for the *Daily Mail*, a journalist had called out Meghan Markle for investing in a product and then sending said product off to her neighbour, Oprah Winfrey, who then shared it with her 19 million followers. A great example of an unfair advantage for a founder — and one that so many of us could only dream of.

Besides being aware of your own unfair advantages, it's also helpful for you to know of others' unfair advantages, so you do not compare yourself to someone who clearly has had a step up. This is something many people don't talk about, instead only telling us about the 'success'. For example, one of the Snapchat co-founders became the youngest billionaire, but he was also brought up in a million-dollar home by well-connected lawyer parents, which gave him access to CEOs of tech companies. Money is not the only unfair advantage; there is also intelligence and insight, location/luck, education/expertise and status.

Are unfair advantages bad? Yes and no. Some are rooted in systems that work against certain communities and some you can create yourself to help you get ahead — I encourage you to do the latter. Unfair advantages give you a competitive advantage and as mentioned before your network is one of them; networks are not easily built, some people are born into them, but you can create your own with a bit of luck and effort.

In 2017, when I moved back to London, I wrote down a list of the people I wanted to connect with. People who I had read about online and seemed to be influencers and decision makers in the spaces I wanted to exist in. I wanted to learn very quickly about the startup world and tap into specific communities. I met these people by connecting with them on social media and attending events they had shared on their platforms. Today, these people are my peers, my most valuable asset and learning from them is what has helped me.

One of those people is Nafisa Bakkar, co-founder of Amaliah. We had first met on Twitter and she was kind enough to give me a call and share advice around seeking a co-founder. She spoke to me about how to decide on shares, how to gain ownership over time (vesting) and how she had built her media company. Having access to founders gives you leverage as you can learn from their own journey and they can also make helpful introductions – there are many benefits!

I have been able to build a solid network of experienced individuals who range from CEOs to marketing experts to investors, which has been helpful and very beneficial to FWL. Thankfully, with the internet we can now network with people all over the world in minutes and create a global network — I call my network my 'power circle'. If you've avoided networking and need the tips on how to make it happen, read on.

WHO TO HAVE IN YOUR POWER CIRCLE

Before you start getting connected, think about who you want or need in your power circle to support your idea and side hustle.

Mentors

An essential part of your power circle are mentors; they come in many different forms and are able to offer valuable advice towards your side hustle. Make use of them by connecting with them regularly and letting them know about your progress. You control the relationship, so don't expect them to chase you, and be respectful of their time.

Here are the types of mentors to consider:

- Traditional mentor: Having people who are more experienced than you in your industry and have an influential say is important for learning from someone's experience and getting a hand up. But as you most probably know, they're likely to be high in demand, which leads me to my next point.
- Peer mentor: If you can't connect to lots of traditional mentors, your next best bet is to gather some peer mentors around you. These are the type of people who have similar years of experience, who are currently at the same stage in life and can provide the regular support with advice and even in helping with projects. It's always nice to grow with people.
- Reverse mentor: These people may be less experienced and also younger, but despite that there is still a lot to learn from this type of mentor. Maybe it could be that they are more experienced in understanding a particular aspect of your business, such as social media, and would offer a good hand in helping you build those skills.

Personal board of advisors

Similar to the board of directors for a company, these groups of people are here to give you advice and support for your professional and personal life in general. They tend to consist of family members, long-time mentors and even friends — people you feel comfortable turning to when you need them. This board is not formalised, and you most probably have this group around you already. The key thing here, in comparison to a board of directors, is that the members of your board don't formally know or sign up — these relationships grow organically. Try to include people with diverse backgrounds and perspectives so that your advice is varied. When I had interviewed Victoria Prew for the entrepreneurial mindset chapter, she reflected on the challenges her business had faced during the pandemic and was grateful that she was able to pull out her phone and reach out to experienced leaders and ask them for advice on pivoting and how to mentally handle the situation.

REFRAME YOUR THINKING ON 'NETWORKING'

To help you get over the hurdle of building your network, reframe your thinking around what it is — it's more than standing around with a drink in your hand in a fancy venue — you are likely to meet people anywhere and everywhere. For me, it means creating 'meaningful connections'. This goes beyond knowing someone's name and having their connection on LinkedIn; it's having a real interest in someone and connecting with that in mind.

NETWORK ^ AND >

As with mentoring, make sure you not only network up but also across. Actress, writer, director, and producer of the

HBO hit series *Insecure,* Issa Rae, shared in a video that in the early days of her career it was 'networking across' that helped her. She said, 'Who's next to you? Who's struggling? Who's in the trenches with you? Who's just as hungry as you are? Those are the people that you need to build with.' She collaborated with peers and was able to create projects that have got her the recognition that has led to her success and more opportunities. Networking across allows you to make new friends and build with people who are also looking for opportunities.

ESTABLISH GOALS

If you're specific about what it is you want to achieve, you can be more intentional and strategic about building your circle. Is it connecting with peers in your field or is it looking for mentors who can advise you on starting a side hustle? Or maybe journalists who are experienced in covering the industry your side hustle is focused on? Whatever the goals are, get clear on them by thinking about what the priorities are for you and your side hustle.

TAKE IT SLOW

As ambitious as you may be, creating genuine connections takes time — whether these connections came through social media or via introductions. Moving from the cold email to an actual, real-life conversation could take a couple of months of effort. Start slowly and commit to connecting with one or two people a month or however many you feel comfortable with. When you connect, start with the personal chit-chat then progress to the professional talk — making sure you find out about what they are working on, how you can support them, then end with your own ask.

SHARE YOUR STORY/INTERESTS

Be vocal about your side hustle and what you're trying to achieve with it — share it with those around you, on social media and however you can. You'd be surprised that you will start attracting the network you want without having to do all the heavy lifting. People like connecting with people who are doing interesting things!

BUILD IT BEFORE YOU NEED IT

Don't wait until you need something to start connecting with someone; no one wants someone reaching out for a favour without having established a connection with them. Of course, this can happen in some instances but I find it's better to connect and build some familiarity way before you need anything. For example, I have a tendency to add people working on interesting things to my LinkedIn — I'll pop them a message complimenting their work and ask them to connect whenever they're free; most of the time there is no intention for an ask. As you begin to share content on your LinkedIn timeline, they'll begin to connect with it, which helps in building a connection for when you may decide to reach out to them.

HOW TO FIND THEM

There are a few ways by which you can find people to connect with to become mentors or to build new connections with.

- Look inside: Start within your own network; thinking of family, friends and colleagues — who could offer advice or who could they connect you with? Social media networks allow you to see mutual contacts, so your first connection could help in making an onward introduction if need be.
- Communities: Join online and real-life communities of people that share the same interests or where your target audience for your side hustle hangs out. A few online communities are YSYS (Your Startup Your Story), The Stack World and Femstreet.
- Social media: From Twitter to LinkedIn to the Dots and also platforms like Lunchclub.ai and Bumble Bizz, digital has given us the opportunity to make connections locally and globally.
- Formal mentorship programmes: Look out for structured mentorship programmes that not only connect you with mentors but also with peer mentors. These types of programmes help to take the pressure off networking.
- Events: Industry and networking events are good places to start, but you never know who you might meet at non-professional events too.

REACHING OUT

Our first instinct when wanting to reach out to people is that they will be too busy or unwilling to help; both can be true, but not always, and I encourage you not to lead with those thoughts. There are people out there who want to help you, who have been where you are or are currently where you are, and the only thing separating the relationship is reaching out.

Read on for how to reach out and create connections online.

Connect the dots

When wanting to reach out to someone, as mentioned before, always check to see if you have mutual contacts — if so, and you're comfortable enough to do so, ask for an introduction. When asking for an introduction via email, write a draft of the email they could potentially send on, which takes most of the effort out of their hands. I have done this in the past and it's a perfect way for you to write your own introduction and put your best foot forward – no one can sell you better than yourself.

Connecting via email

If you haven't already connected on other social platforms, email is likely to be the first point of interaction between you and the person you want to connect with. Here are some tips that will help in getting you a response.

- Use plugins: Use Contact Out to help you find the preferred emails for the people you want to approach via LinkedIn or search online in Google, or on their social media platforms.
- Professional emails only: Make sure you are sending from a professional email address, preferably one that includes the domain of your side hustle. Domain emails are so simple to set up these days. I personally use Gmail for business.
- Let the subject line say it all: This is one of the first things the recipient sees before deciding to open an email. Instead of writing something vague such as 'connecting', be more clear and to the point with something like 'Can we discuss my new side hustle?' Asking a question will make the reader curious.
- Customise the sender name: If you want to mention your business name as well as your name, for instance, do; I have 'Elizabeth, For Working Ladies'. This seems more personal than just your business name.
- Follow up: Never assume people are ignoring you — they are probably just very busy, especially if they are a public figure. It's likely they are high in demand. Give it about a week before you follow up the second time, then try one more time.

How the email flow should look:

- A greeting
- Introduction to who you are
- Why you are connecting with them

- Pay a compliment to their work
- Suggest a proposed time and day to connect online or IRL. You could even take another step and share an online calendar with your availability.

Everything above should be 1–2 lines each; keep the email short and snappy. I tend to get overwhelmed when I see a long email from a stranger.

Social media

Social media offers a fantastic platform to approach others, but always do so with courtesy, just as you would via email.

- Engage first: An easy way to connect with someone on social media is by engaging with their content, for instance, replying and liking their tweets or re-sharing their work on LinkedIn.
- To DM or not to DM: Some people like this and some people don't; in most cases people will let you know via their bio if you should keep all work-related info via email. If there is no clue, I tend to send a DM and ask if they are open to discussing what I had in mind via DM.

Taking it offline

I love the online world, but give me the opportunity to drop my phone and meet people offline and I'd take it in a heartbeat. Meeting people in real life allows you to truly authentically connect, and this experience cannot be replicated through technology. When setting up time to connect, make sure you take the lead and do the following things:

- Considering you have a full-time job, find time to meet either early before work, during your lunch break or after work. Whatever you decide on, allow enough time for the commute so you are not late for work or your meeting.
- Put it in their diary: Help them keep organised and put it top of their mind so they don't forget.
- Select a location that is more suitable for them: I always tend to want my connections to travel less, so I choose somewhere that is more convenient for them.
- Map out the conversation: Have in mind the way you'd like the conversation to go, as this will allow you to be prepared and manage the time better. So make sure you have your asks ready, if there are any. That being said, give room to be flexible, too.

MANAGING RELATIONSHIPS

Whether it be mentors, a personal board of advisors or new contacts, investing time into managing the connections you have is vital to keeping those connections strong. Depending on your last discussion or the role the connection plays in your life, regular email updates would be great. For example, if you discussed with your mentor the challenge of getting your side hustle off the ground and gave them a deadline for launch, then you can agree to update them every two weeks with the action you have taken. This not only holds you accountable but makes your mentor feel included, as if they are being carried along. For those that may just be contacts in your network, check-ins on how they are doing via email can also be helpful.

GIVE BACK AND KEEP CONNECTING THE DOTS

Be ready to say more than 'thank you' and to add genuine value by supporting your new contacts in any way possible. Ask them what you could do to support their own projects or goals, or if there is anyone you could help connect them with; connections are a two-way street and both parties should benefit.

GET TO WORK

1. If you were to throw an intimate gathering, who would you want in the room? Make that list.
2. Create a plan for how you will reach out to them and give yourself a deadline.
3. Who in your contact list could make an introduction to your dream guest list? Ask them for introductions.
4. Write down and get clear on the goal of connecting with these people.

NICOLE CRENTSIL

Founder & CEO of Black Girl Festival and Bigsis.co, Angel Investor and Board Member

WHO IS NICOLE CRENTSIL?

Nicole is a Ghanaian–British cultural curator, creative consultant and entrepreneur based in London. In 2018, Forbes listed Nicole as one of 100 women to follow on Twitter and LinkedIn. In the same year, Time Out named Nicole as one of 50 Londoners shaping the city's cultural landscape. Nicole is the CEO of Black Girl Festival, a platform dedicated to Black women, girls and non-binary people. She's also the founder of BIG SIS, a platform dedicated to supporting the personal development of creative working women. Nicole is passionate about connecting women, young people and underrepresented groups to art, culture and events.

NICOLE'S STORY

In 2016, I started my first project — I guess my first side hustle – which was Unmasked Women. Unmasked was about the desire to see more conversations about Black women and our mental health, specifically with the experiences that we have in the UK. I had seen and read a few articles about African–American women and was also going through my own period of depression and I wasn't too sure where or which communities were having this conversation. So I created this project, really just as a means to express how I was feeling and to create a support network with other creatives who might have felt the same way. That led to actually launching an exhibition, which I guess was my first actual practice of gaining community support or really thinking about money from a sustainable perspective and how it can support your side project or a hustle.

The exhibition was initially self-funded; I saved up some money from my full-time job and put it towards the exhibition. I was working with an organisation that supported creatives in finding venues for their projects. I was introduced to a venue called The Artworks but didn't hear back for weeks, only to find that my main contact had quit and they were no longer supporting creatives in this capacity. From that initial email introduction I basically stalked the The Artworks, noticed they were hiring, hustled my way into getting a job and in my first week said, 'Do you remember being introduced to me over email about my Unmasked Women project? Well, I'd love to host it here,' and they said YES! lol. So I wiggled my way in when it seemed like I was losing my opportunity. The event went well – I produced a press release to gain coverage, charged for tickets and I reinvested everything from the ticket sales back into covering the costs of the actual exhibition. I also invested in a local mental health charity, hired two interns and paid for their internship through this side hustle.

In 2017 I co-founded Black Girl Festival – the UK's first festival celebrating Black British women and girls. At BGF, I really expanded on everything that I'd already learned in 2016; it was basically a mega version of Unmasked Women — just 10 times the scale. It was really exciting because it was something that was the first of its kind at the time. And we were also relying on the fact that it was the first in the UK on this scale. It was something that we had never really seen before, that the community actually needed to bring us all together, to bring different partners, collectives, creatives, media platforms all into one space.

To make BGF a reality, we decided to start a crowdfunder. The crowdfunder was relying on people to really understand the idea and see the need for it to exist, for them to make that initial investment. It was really successful. We had such great feedback and response on our social media channels and on the crowdfunding platform. In the first week of the crowdfunding going live, the crowdfunding UK co-founders reached out to us, they were really impressed with the analytics. They just saw the engagement on their back end and were confident the crowdfunder would work out well. We set up a meeting with them at a Starbucks at Victoria, and they took the time to share valuable advice — they were keen to support us, which got us excited. I thought, 'Oh my gosh. This must mean we might be on to something here.' The timeline of what we were doing was about seven weeks; four weeks to raise the money, then three weeks to programme the whole thing and create all of it from scratch. So, there was a lot of pressure. I was working full-time, it happened really quickly but also it was just all really exciting!

We raised awareness about the crowdfunder through social media, mainly Instagram and Twitter, and our message focused on the intentions we had for BGF. The platform always recommends you have a fun, engaging video to explain what you are *raising funds for and how you plan to use them. However, we didn't have the time to create a savvy video, and instead we were relying on social media to do its magic – we continuously asked the community, our friends and our networks to share with their networks, our mums in their WhatsApp group chats — literally just everyone and anyone. Initially we had one piece of PR coverage, sharing the vision of BGF and what to expect from us. They couldn't mention the crowdfunding campaign but had agreed to cover it if we were successful and ran the event — so we'd get post-event press coverage. So we thought, 'Okay, well, we'll just rely on our community and just get everyone else to share it and really hype it up.' That was more or less our strategy.*

From 2017 up until 2020, everything was really on a project-by-project basis. I went freelance at the end of 2018/the beginning of 2019. This was when things started really picking up, but after you crowdfund for that side hustle, and you pay everyone – you pay all the contributors, the venue, you cover all the costs – you're sitting there with zero in your account, right? You want to do it again but you don't want to rely on the community as heavily to make it possible. I started reflecting on everything that we had done, and thought, 'This is not just a side hustle, this is not just a project, this could actually be a fully fledged business.' So it was really about figuring out a sustainable business model, and taking it from being a side hustle to being a business, and thinking about how we could continue to reinvest everything back into the business that will likely go back into our community. Could we work as an agency? Could we work as events-based business? And not only thinking about what would make the biggest impact but also what would make us money — putting the money back into making this bigger and better each year.

We initially discarded the option of seeking funding – our type of company would approach something like Arts Council England but the process was just laborious. We then took the idea to an arts institution, who had said we would need to remove the name 'Black Girl', because they feared it was isolating a community. At that point, we said to ourselves, 'Okay, we're just going to crowdfund this because we're not going to rely on other people who will eventually tear it apart and make it something that it's not.' After the first festival and going forward, we made a commitment that what we're not doing is ever compromising on who we are and our community and what we're trying to do. And that meant that we have to be independent, self-sufficient and also profitable. I remember I had a really great conversation with one of my founder friends, who shared some advice when I was dancing around the idea of potentially getting VC investment or even just understanding what that whole world is about – he encouraged me not to go down that route just yet. He said, 'No, don't do that. If you're making money, just focus on making money and keep reinvesting it.'

It's a real hustle.

Yeah, so we're still self-funded and completely reinvesting everything that we've got and just taking a massive risk, as many people do. You take the risk when you hire people, you take the risk when you try new things, so it's having the courage to take that risk into saying, okay, we're gonna place a bet on our community and try to create as much as we can for that community and develop these products and services to ensure that we see our community thriving. Some funding would be great, though.

Starting this side hustle has brought about so many opportunities for me. I guess my ability to amass and engage the community has done wonders. It has opened a lot of doors. The most recent one being becoming an angel investor for Ada Venture, knowing that there is such an incredible community of Black women, who are founders, many first-time founders, who are looking for investment but also who are looking for better access to knowledge about this whole ecosystem, this world, the next stage and about investing. I am in the best position to support these women, as I straddle between the founder/investor remit, but that's really exciting because it means I can also see both sides.

Creating this platform, being a founder, creating a community-first business also helped me in terms of the work that I do and the investments I want to make. They just work hand in hand and it makes so much sense for me to work in that avenue. I have also been given the opportunity to sit on a few boards. The future is exciting and I'm glad to be able to contribute to the growth of Black women.

NICOLE'S WORDS OF WISDOM

- Whether you want to start a business or a crowdfunder, make sure to be community first. Focus and home in on what your community needs, getting yourself engaged with conversations and topics and discussions, really on what the community is talking about. The best way for crowdfunding campaigns to take off is when they are community-focused.

- Every side hustle does not need to become a fully-fledged business. Not everyone wants to work for themselves, not everyone wants to quit their job and do this full time. And also, not everyone has that entrepreneurial spirit or drive to be able to carry this on; nobody should go down the route of forcing themselves to become a founder because the journey is not easy and it's not fun. We're crazy people . . .

- Enjoy the ride. Enjoy every aspect of making that side hustle work, literally, it's in the name: 'hustling'. It's making connections, making things work, working ad hoc. It's DIY. It's really just experimenting and playing around with stuff and enjoying that time; I feel like that essence sometimes gets lost, because people want to make a quick buck and start making big, big money and getting investors and it's like 'No, keep a side hustle as a side hustle and enjoy that process.'

@nkrystal_
@blackgirlfest
blackgirlfest.com

YOUR HEALTH, THE MOST IMPORTANT ASSET

'Your side hustle is not worth it, if it puts your health on the line.'

Gone are the days where we have conversations about work and business and don't prioritise health. A few years ago it was a battle between hustling hard or getting more sleep, now the latter has become a priority and we are starting to look at how we can work and live better in order to operate to the best of our ability. There's a myth that if you work a job that you are passionate about you won't spend a day working — who the hell came up with that? Regardless of passion, we are working and we get tired, and when we do we should feel no guilt about wanting to rest. If you're reading this, you're likely to be an ambitious high-achiever, always wanting to *do more*, and that's fine, but not at the detriment of your wellbeing.

As mentioned previously, in the early days of running FWL I was managing over 20 writers, interviewing women for features and editing. I did all this while also promoting the content on a daily basis and running another business. I was determined to see my idea come alive, and seeing the traction it was gaining fuelled me even more. I sometimes receive emails asking if FWL is 'hiring', and it makes me chuckle because there is an assumption that there is a team running the platform. People tend to think I'm crazy when they realise it's just me. Of course, after a year or two this couldn't last, I started asking for help. I realised that the quality was dropping because I was burning out and I just felt completely unproductive – the worst feeling ever. I couldn't enjoy the work I was doing, and so I vowed to myself that I'd never trade my health for work again.

Running a side hustle will require you to put in a few extra hours. But working those longer hours and not getting the results you want from your side hustle – or not getting them as quickly as you'd like – could lead to physical and mental fatigue. Yes, this journey can be fun and the thought of seeing an idea take off can make us willing to burn the midnight oil, but prevention is better than cure, and prioritising your health from early on will save you having to disrupt the progress of your side hustle due to burnout.

Here are a few ways to manage your health as you pursue this journey.

COMMUNITY

When starting a new business we naturally tend to turn into hermits, keep the idea a secret and work alone. This is because we fear someone will steal our ideas or we just get carried away and throw ourselves into our work. However, this can bring a sense of loneliness and this in itself is not healthy, even if you claim to be an introvert. A study conducted by the University of Chicago[1] found that people who feel lonely are likely to have less-effective immune systems – being around others can help in combating this. Which means being around others can help in keeping you healthy.

Here are a few ways to stay connected:

Connecting the dots

These days there are many ways to connect with communities, whether they are online or offline, and they are a good way for you to build your network. You could attend regular community meet-ups, or just connect with communities on social channels such as Instagram or Twitter. Feeling connected to others is healthy and also a good way to learn and share challenges that you may be facing with your side hustle. When thinking of these communities, keep in mind that you want to connect with people who are at similar stages as you so you can discuss relatable topics.

Accountability partner or squad

Checking in with someone or a group not only allows you to keep on top of your to-dos but can also lift your mood. When creating this accountability relationship, make sure you schedule in recurring meetings. For instance, you could decide to

---

[1] https://www.ncbi.nlm.nih.gov/pubmed/20652462?source=post_page

chat on a weekly basis on a particular day, or maybe once every two weeks. Try different options and stick to what works for you. You can find paid membership accountability groups online or choose someone in your immediate circle to start with.

Your female friendships are the energy you need

When it comes to fighting off anxiety, your female friendships are the cure. A lecture given at Stanford University on the mind–body connection by Dr David Spiegel,[2] Professor of Psychiatry, found that women who nurture their friendships with their female friends were healthier than those who don't. Us women have a way of connecting soul to soul and speaking with our emotions. The quality time we spend with our female friends helps to create more serotonin, a neurotransmitter that helps combat depression and can promote a general feeling of wellbeing.[3] It's that time spent telling your girls how great they are, having a laugh about the ups and downs of life or just having the shoulder to cry on that makes you happy and brightens your day. The professor suggested that spending time with your female friends is just as important as going to the gym. Spending time chit-chatting with friends is not a waste of time, it is beneficial to your health, so dedicate time to your girls.

---

[2] http://stresshealthcenter.stanford.edu/

[3] https://thriveglobal.com/stories/girlfriends-are-good-for-your-health/

MIND

It all starts on the inside, so here are a few easy ways to keep your mind healthy.

Journaling[4]

There are different types of journaling, which serve so many purposes. It is a great practice for anyone looking to feel less overwhelmed. Writing down your thoughts, your feelings, goals and achievements not only allows you to track your life but to also identify, confront and diminish negative thoughts and emotions while enhancing your sense of wellbeing. Writing things down allows you to clear mental blocks, calm your mind, know yourself better and, most importantly, it is a great stress-management tool. The best thing about your journal is that it is non-judgemental; it takes you as you are, so be open and write freely. I'd advise doing this when you wake up and just before bed, as this helps clear your mind, taking away any sort of overwhelm that you may be experiencing so you are in the right mindset to sleep or get started on your day.

Gratitude journaling

An extension of journaling is gratitude journaling. I came across this concept a few years ago when I read an article about sending a text each day to someone that you wanted to thank. Not only did this remind me that I have good people around me

---

[4] https://thedoctorweighsin.com/can-journaling-improve-your-mental-health/

but also that I have things to be thankful for. Gratitude won't always come to you naturally because we are always on the go and looking for the next thing, which is why setting time aside to practise it will help you cultivate gratitude more naturally. Gratitude journaling is simply expressing appreciation for the things you have learnt or experienced, including anything good in your life not just now, but also to come. This practice can help lift your spirit and bring your mind into a much more positive space; it allows you to reflect on the goodness in your life.

Meditating

As with journaling, there are many purposes and types of meditation, and the aim here is to achieve a feeling of relaxation and inner peace. If you'd rather not try guided or spiritual meditation, there is the option of just learning to sit still and focus your mind for a few minutes a day. As you begin to practise each day you will find you are able to meditate for longer. This shouldn't only be restricted to the morning but whenever you need to relax your mind, or you could block out the best time for you during the day. It is also really helpful to do before a big occasion.

Therapy

Whether you decide to start a side hustle or are occupied with your current job, any type of work can bring a lot of stress, especially in a high-pressure environment, so considering therapy for support is a good call. Therapy provides professional mental support as opposed to the support you get from an accountability group or talking to friends. The rate of those who start a business and become stressed is rather high, because they tend to be high achievers and place a large amount of expectation on themselves.

Coaching/mentoring

Mentoring and coaching are quite different, but they will both provide you with mental support as you embark on something new. Mentoring is focused on giving you guidance and advice based on the person's experience, while coaching tends to be focused on a particular thing that you want to achieve. For example, there are coaches that focus on teaching you how to use digital marketing for sales or simply how to become a better salesperson. Having these types of people around you takes the burden off your shoulders in not having to figure things out by yourself. However, it's important that you identify whether you need a mentor or a coach in order to set realistic expectations.

BODY

Our bodies are sacred and we shouldn't wait for illness to occur before we start treating them right.

Staying active

Regular exercise reduces your levels of stress and anxiety and can make your mind more alert. It does not have to be anything radical, it could just be something light, such as taking a brisk walk or run, as long as you increase your heart rate.

Physical activity triggers a release of dopamine and serotonin, which can improve mood, and this one activity can lead to a series of other positive habits, such as eating nutritious foods, sleeping well and drinking fluids regularly. It is recommended that we participate in at least 2.5 hours of moderate aerobic activity a week, or 75 minutes of more vigorous activity. This shouldn't be too difficult to fit in – make sure it's something you enjoy and find ways to make it fun by mixing up the activities or joining in with groups, whether that be through community-focused sport brands such as ClassPass or Peloton or at classes at your local gym.

Food for wellbeing

The quality of the food we eat can help in making a day go from feeling like it's a drag to feeling highly productive – that is the power of what we put into our bodies. I won't preach the whole 'clean eating' idea to you, because I believe anything can be eaten as long as it is part of a balanced diet. However, do prioritise the foods that help your mental health, especially during working hours. Foods such as fruits, green leafy veg, nuts and lean proteins have all been found to increase our feelings of wellbeing.[5]

Sleep

This subject has become an important matter that we are now beginning to pay attention to – and rightfully so. Getting good sleep is the best thing we could do for our bodies, and

---

[5] https://www.mentalhealth.org.uk/a-to-z/d/diet-and-mental-health

although I believe we have started prioritising sleep, what we do need to consider is what is the optimum time to get better sleep.

So does it matter when we sleep? Yes, we should be heading to get to sleep between 8pm and midnight; once it gets past midnight your body struggles to get real rest. According to sleepfoundation.org, it's best to sleep as much as possible during hours of darkness. Sleeping at night helps align the body's internal clock with its environment.

There have been moments in my life when I have struggled with sleep due to my mind being overworked and stressed, and on these occasions pink noise has really helped. Pink noises are natural sounds like falling rain or the ocean, and not only does this help you fall asleep, it also makes you feel more rested as it slows and regulates the brain waves. Why not try out Insight Timer for a selection of pink noise, and if you can't access the app, try YouTube for some free options.

CREATING A PRODUCTIVE WORK SPACE

We don't think about it much, but what happens outside your head is just as important as what happens inside it – mental health can be impacted by both. Physical environments such as your space at home or at work can directly impact our psychological health, so it's important we recognise the type of surroundings that will help us thrive and better our health.

Clutter

A 2010 study in the *Journal of Personality and Social Psychology*[6] found that women's wellbeing was more likely to be negatively impacted by clutter than men; they found that it can also increase levels of cortisol, a stress hormone. Don't overdo it with the spring cleaning but do be mindful that a clutter-free space has great psychological benefits. Set aside a day a week that you devote to making your space clear and relaxing.

Brighten it up[7]

Whether it be poor natural lighting due to winter or poor interior lighting, both can affect your mood and lead to stress and anxiety, especially in high-pressure environments. A research report by the UK company Staples shares that better lighting makes people happier. To help create a well-lit environment figure out how to provide lighting that imitates natural daylight such as full-spectrum light bulbs which mimic natural light. Items such as a SAD (seasonal affective disorder) lamp could also be helpful. Try to also avoid filling your rooms with dark tones and instead focus on more white or eggshell – as this helps to reflect light in the room – or use mirrors to reflect light.

---

[6] https://www.ncbi.nlm.nih.gov/pubmed/20053034

[7] https://www.forbes.com/sites/pragyaagarwaleurope/2018/12/31/how-does -lighting-affect-mental-health-in-the-workplace/?sh=5e1c215d4ccd

Get green[8]

Plant mum or not, having plants in your environment can play a significant role in making one feel calm and relaxed, thus reducing anxiety. Certain plants can help increase attentiveness and memory, spark creativity and increase productivity. There are also plants that can help with indoor air pollution and consume toxins – top recommendations are bamboo plants and spider plants, which are both safe if you have pets or kids.

If you don't have much space for plants, you could look into purchasing an air filter.

LOOK AT YOUR WORK–LIFE BALANCE

Although I don't truly believe in the concept of work-life balance, we can find healthier ways to do our work. Set yourself a few 'rules' to divide your life and make sure your work and your side hustle don't take over.

Have a hobby and keep it as that

Hobbies aren't just for those who live quiet and relaxed lives, they're for everyone and are a great way to help you disconnect from work and the busyness of life. Research shows that people with hobbies are less likely to suffer from stress, low mood and depression. Make sure you set aside time for your

---

[8] https://www.healthline.com/health/mental-health/plants-self-care#Caring-for-your-plants-is-essentially-a-reminder-to-care-for-yourself

hobbies and keep them sacred and just for your enjoyment; your hobby does not need to be your side hustle.

Social media detox

Self-comparison, getting cancelled, big announcements, the endless scrolling and the list goes on – so has social media brought us any good? Of course it has, but an overload of it can lead to poor mental health. Try to create a healthy relationship with technology. That may mean turning off notifications, signing out of social accounts and limiting your usage on a daily basis, and making sure you do something else, such as spend time with friends, exercise or enjoy your hobby.

Routine

Taking care of you should be a regular practice and not something you do as a result of burnout – prevention is better than cure. Think of ways you can include some type of self-care into your lifestyle. The key times to do some mental wellbeing activities are first thing in the morning and last thing in the evening.

When working a full-time job, you have a schedule — there's a starting and finishing time in which you work specific hours a day — so incorporate a schedule into your side hustle, too, and stick to it.

*

Remember these are suggestions, so I encourage you to try them out and then reflect on what truly works for you.

GET TO WORK

1. Try journaling for 20 minutes at the start of each day or just before you go to bed — to make things easier you could decide to pick a theme for the week or month.
2. Create a routine that prioritises your mental health; list activities that you like and are helpful to you. Try this for a week and make notes on how you feel.
3. Take stock of your current working environment and ask yourself how you can create a better workspace that can impact your wellbeing; for example, how can you reduce the clutter around you?
4. Go to bed an hour earlier this week and try to leave your electronics out of the bedroom.

HAYET RIDA

Strategist at Facebook, Author, Blogger/Influencer and serial side hustler (5 on the go)

WHO IS HAYET RIDA?

Hayet has been a serial side hustler for over 12 years, who currently has five projects on the go, ranging from an educational platform to a luxury candle business. She recently became an author of the children's book One Day They Will Stare. Alongside her side hustle she works as a full-time Creative Strategist at Facebook.

HAYET'S STORY

The inspiration behind starting my side hustles is really the fact that I come up with ideas and I don't fear trying them. I'm not scared of failing because every one that I fail in, I learn something from. That's the secret – not being scared to fail or lose money – but note that I also have steady income from a full-time job.

I started my first side hustle after my first job out of college, which was in an ad agency. My sister had been speaking to a friend that needed a logo for their brand (Christie brand) and I replied, 'I can try.' I had never made a logo in my life but I had thoughts on how it could look. I made this logo in PowerPoint, which they still use today. From then I started creating logos and websites for people and I realised that I liked this, so I started thinking what I could do next.

I never give myself permission to say, 'No, I don't have time,' I give myself time. It's like a boy you like asking if you're free on a Friday night, you most probably aren't but all of a sudden you find time to make yourself free so you can see him. Use this same energy for your side hustle. You will find time if you want to; now when you don't like a boy, you're of course busy!

I have failed many times because I lacked passion for the side hustles. For example, I once created a fitness blog where I was trying out to be a chef and write a cookbook, but I didn't realise until late that I actually really disliked it. Everyone had told me to do it, that I had the potential, but I didn't have the passion and you need passion and hunger to drive you to start something.

I do have a large social community, which has helped me launch my side hustles. I have just over 100,000 followers, which has grown over the last couple of years. In terms of building the audience, I never set out to do this, I just wanted to put my story out there. Imagine going to a town centre and the performer goes to the town clock with all the birds flying around; he performs and people come and go. There are also times when there's probably no one there but he keeps performing – those that like what he's doing will stop and most probably come back every day. This is how you build an audience: you have to go somewhere with something to say with the confidence that no matter if anyone shows up, you'll keep doing it because it's part of your purpose. This is how brands also build their audience, with something to say.

For most people it's their full-time job that has been beneficial to their side hustles, but for me it's the other way round. My side hustles have been beneficial to the work I do in my full-time job because I test and learn things while doing them; whatever works I'll take the learnings and experience to work meetings. Having several side hustles and a team means there are people I'm managing and leading; in my 9–5 I learn from people with regards to how to be a better leader, how to manage time well and have difficult conversations with clients.

My journey of building a team is unique and it's taken me five years to get the best team. I'd say it's important to understand your personality and the types of people you need around you. The best team I've built was from people I've trusted, the people that come to do the work and want to move the business forward. A lot of people are attracted to work with me because I'm an influencer and they want to see what the glamorous life is really like, but I need doers.

In terms of managing your team with a full-time job, you must learn to set clear boundaries. I've told my team on several occasions that 'if the world is not burning, do not contact me during the day'. I also only hire side hustlers: they understand that we are limited by time and know how to manage it. We are all so concise with how we work and review better ways of working.

For those that run side hustles, we need to make sure not to burn out and something that has helped me is focusing on what is in front of me. It's like planning to run a marathon, you're either going to be stressed out by the fact that you have to run 26 miles or you're going to say, 'I have to run 3 miles today and tomorrow 3.5 miles.' I focus on what I need to do today, the things that will get me closer to my goal.

I'm known for 'getting it done' but what people don't see is that I don't have much of a social life. My friends know what it's like and they understand that – if they don't it will be hard. If I'm going to an event, I'm going for one hour because I have a shoot in the morning, if I'm hanging with a friend then we might choose to make it a work hangout. You can do all you desire to do but you will need to cut out some things in order to do everything. I also create moments where I fully let go, no work or anything else, just holiday and enjoyment, but that isn't my full-time life.

If we are honest with ourselves, the most beneficial things about having a side hustle are money, safety, stability and the ability to guarantee my rent, insurance or even capital to start a new venture.

HAYET RIDA'S WORDS OF WISDOM

- Look after your mental health by creating activities where you are pouring back into yourself; for me, that's going to therapy twice a week. I need it because I wouldn't be able to balance everything; therapy helps me work through other mental things so I have space to be productive.

- Find ways that help you stay productive; for me that's a list of things that need to get done only for today. I'd also add that you should be very specific with those things that you want to do and when you want to get them done. For example: reply to Natalie's email on availability by 11am.
- Just start it, start your side hustles and don't ask anyone's opinion, that's the mistake we normally make. When you have an idea, your biggest disservice is asking people if you should do it; they'll likely respond with what they'd do versus it being right for you. If you fail, that's fine, you at least tried.

@hayetrida
@ridabookco
@aiyacandle
@theridacollective

BETTER WAYS OF WORKING

'To improve your working life, the best thing you can do for yourself is get to know thyself.'

Does work–life balance truly exist? Can we separate work from our personal lives, especially as someone running a side hustle? Do longer hours mean better results? Do productivity hacks really work? It's all debatable, but what we can do is find better ways of working by understanding how we work best. This could lead to less burnout and increased productivity. Choosing to pursue a side hustle means working extra hours – which may be earlier mornings, evenings or weekends – and this is something you'll have to get used to while you learn and figure out how and when you work best. Read on for some tips to help you boost your productivity.

KNOW THYSELF

Becoming self-aware gives you data about yourself. And in this instance you need data on your productivity, and how and what makes you work better. Asides from journaling your feelings, you can also take personality tests that reveal your best working styles and motivators. For example, something like the Myers-Briggs test. Things you should be looking out for include:

- What drains you?
- What energises you?
- When is your most productive time of the day?
- How do you best like to work?
- Which tasks slow you down?

This data will help you assist yourself in working better and being more efficient so you can plan on setting realistic deadlines. As I am mildly dyslexic, I am more aware that it may take me double the time of the average person to read a book – this is fine, as I then do not set unrealistic expectations of myself – but I only know this through having observed myself.

ENERGY MAPPING

This is focused on understanding your energy. What restores your energy and what depletes it? Every task and activity we do throughout the day will do either one. Creating an energy map allows you to effectively create an environment and day in which you can thrive. Below are the headers you could use for your energy map, with some examples.

People (friends, family, colleagues, network, etc.)

- Restores: Simone (new founder friend, checks in on how my side hustle is doing)
- Depletes: Becky (always negative and doubts me)

Activities

- Restores: Netball
- Depletes: Phone calls after 9pm

Work

- Restores: Connecting with customers at community events
- Depletes: Event planning

In cases where you realise your energy is being depleted but the responsibility, activity, etc., cannot be avoided, try to think of times when you have high energy and will be able to cope better. For example, if email admin depletes your energy you can either outsource this task to a virtual assistant or think of a time in the day where your energy is high and you are likely to get through this activity easily.

DON'T RELY ON MOTIVATION

Some say that in order to get productive and get things done, you need motivation. Honestly, if we could all be motivated every day that would be an absolute dream, but we all know that is not the case – it is just not realistic. Motivation is fleeting, here today and gone tomorrow – rather like an unfaithful friend. No matter how much you believe in what you are doing, sometimes you just want to do nothing, and whether that's a form of burnout you're experiencing or just an odd day, the point remains that while motivation is nice to have, we cannot always rely on it to help us achieve our goals. Instead, focus on building habits that help you get to your goals and understand what drives you to take action. For me, that is accountability and being intentional with everyday tasks.

Finally, start small – do the bare minimum to get you started, then increase this over time; radicalness does not always bring consistency. For example, if you need to post on social media to build a relationship with your customers, start with doing this two days a week and become consistent with this before increasing it to four days a week. It's all about the small adjustments.

WORK SMART, NOT HARD

There is nothing fancy about being a workaholic, and working long, hard hours does not equal results, and most times it even delivers more problems. Figure out the most efficient way of getting things done whatever the task may be. If you have this approach in mind you will always be seeking out the fastest and most efficient methods as to how you can reduce tasks and steps. Work smart, not hard.

SCHEDULING TASKS

With limited time to work on your side hustle, it's important that you plan and schedule your tasks in advance. Plan out what needs to be done, how long each task will take and how long you have to complete it. This will help you create a more realistic schedule.

Bullet journaling

This tool requires pen and paper, and for that reason it has become a favourite of mine! Instead of writing a long to-do list, try the bullet journaling system created by Ryder Carroll. The Bullet Journal® method organises scheduling, reminders, to-do lists and anything else that you need to plan ahead for, all in a notebook in different sections. The diary does not come in template and requires you to design it as you please, according to your goals and needs. You can complete this for the year, month, week and day. I have customised my own bullet journal to focus on weeks and days, with sections on my days that include emails that need to be sent and people that need to be called as sections. You should aim to fill this out at the beginning of the week and the beginning of the day, or the night before. Do a quick google of the different options out there or visit www.bulletjournal.com for more info.

Deep focused work

Deep work has been a life-saver for me; in a world full of distractions focus is harder to achieve now than ever before.

Cal Newport defines deep work as 'focused, uninterrupted, undistracted work on a task that pushes your cognitive abilities to their limit'. This is prioritising the highest-value tasks. To truly get your side hustle off the ground with limited hours to work on it, you'll need to develop the ability to shut out distractions and focus less on the shallow work that we tend to do when distracted. Newport defines shallow work as 'minor duties performed in a state of distractions', such as checking emails, attending unnecessary meetings or WhatsApping. It's great to have the intention to do deep work but what are the practical steps you can take?

- Make it a ritual and block out a set amount of time. For example, you may limit this to 2 hours an evening from 7–9pm, or a whole day at the weekend, or maybe do deep work in the morning and shallow work in the evening – whichever tends to work best for you. Newport advises that the maximum amount of deep work to be achieved in a day, even by experts, should be four hours.
- Take out all distractions: this could be switching off your device, turning off notifications, turning off the internet, avoiding switching between tasks – whatever the rules are, make sure you follow them in order to have pure undiluted focus.

Focus is like a muscle and you must train it by repeating it again and again, which will allow it to become stronger. So maybe start with 30 minutes of deep work instead of one hour and gradually increase this over time. Don't worry if you get distracted in the first couple of sessions, just try to really minimise those distractions and bring your focus back to what you were working on. I sometimes ask a friend to check in on me after sessions to discuss what I accomplished and how I feel, which has helped me to reflect on my working behaviour.

Calls and meetings

My stance on this is: if it's not in my diary then it's not happening – I just won't remember. Schedule all calls and meetings in your diary so you can plan ahead, be prepared and also know how much time you have left for other tasks; remember, this is a side hustle so you have limited time. Make sure to set reminders about these calls. I set two reminders, which typically tend to be a day before and one hour before, through Google calendar but you could also consider using a scheduling tool like Calendly.

GET THE BIG THINGS OUT OF THE WAY

Our intuition will always naturally tell us to choose the small and easy tasks when we have a list of items to complete, but we should aim to get the biggest tasks (highest value) out of the way first. These tend to be the ones we procrastinate about but that also have the highest value in terms of output. We like completing the easiest tasks as we get a sense of immediate satisfaction from them and feel like we are progressing, but what could be happening is that our difficult tasks just continue to pile up. In order to still experience this feeling of satisfaction with the big, difficult tasks we should break these down into bite-size actions and tackle them step by step. Smaller tasks can be delegated or outsourced, so don't get caught up in the little things. Tasks such as fixing a bug on your website could be solved by hiring an expert freelancer online.

MORNING POWER

Mornings are when our brains are well rested, providing we went to sleep on time and slept well, so dedicating your morning to some top-level important tasks such as planning ahead makes the most sense. This doesn't necessarily mean you have to wake up at 5am, just that we should use our mornings for the important things. Research has also shown that exercising in the morning provides energy and boosts your motivation, which in turn leads to an increase of productivity. Use your mornings wisely.

MULTITASKING

The myth of multitasking serves no one and leads to a lack of productivity; it's better to compartmentalise tasks into set times than to jump from task to task during one period. How do you decide which one gets completed first? How do you decide what has priority?

If you struggle to decide what is a priority, then the Eisenhower Matrix is a useful technique for you to try. It helps you decide on the work that is a priority. Below is the matrix divided into four quadrants, which makes it simple and straightforward to use. While you list all your tasks, you can begin to note whether they are important or urgent according to the matrix.

SET EFFECTIVE GOALS

Goal-setting is a powerful tool in creating focus for yourself and providing guidance on what needs to be worked on. This helps to improve your productivity as you have something tangible to strive towards. When starting out on a side hustle there are so many things that need to be done and you're likely to be doing them all yourself.

Set out a clear vision from the beginning and create a strategy that will help you get there. Then begin to work backwards into yearly, quarterly, monthly and daily goals, which are all broken down into actionable steps. As you go along, it's important that you check in on whether those goals are still the best way forward, as you may come across information that now makes the goals unrealistic or no longer accurate.

Criteria for a good goal

Specific: Clearly defined; there should be no doubt about what you are trying to achieve.

Measurable: You should be able to measure progress and have a clear indication of when your goal has been reached.

Achievable: Attainable and not impossible to achieve. Make sure you have the resources required.

Realistic: Is this goal within reach? Have you given yourself enough time?

Time-bound: Give a start date and end date for this goal.

SMART goals set you up for success and hold you accountable, whereas goals that are not SMART lead to failure.

Examples of SMART goals

Non-SMART goal: I want to increase my sales.

SMART goal: I want to make 100 product sales by 30 January and to do so I will send out two email campaigns a month.

A goal-setting method

A method for goal setting is Objectives and Key Results (OKRs), which was created by Andy Grove. This method can be used for both your personal life and side hustle.

OKRs make it clear what you want to achieve and provide measurable outcomes. The objective should give a clear goal. What are the outcomes of achieving the objectives and what would the results look like? The key results will tell you the most important things that will help you hit your objective.

Example

Objective: Grow leicour.com membership to 100 members by December 2021.

Key result:

- Secure three pieces of press coverage in industry publications.
- Speak at three industry events.
- Pitch to a minimum of 50 potential clients.
- Collaborate/partner with five communities with the same target audience.

When it is time for you to check in on your goals, measure each one using the following scale to mark what you have achieved: You measure each goal by using the following scale:

On a scale of 0–1.0

0 = no progress

0.3 = made some progress but did not meet the key results

0.7 = achieved key result

1.0 = accomplished more than that key result, e.g. grew membership to 150 members

I like this goal-setting method because you are able to track progress, it's not a hard 'did not achieve' or 'achieved'. You should have a max of six OKRs and set them as you desire; this could be monthly or quarterly.

WRITE A DONE LIST

As a to-do list would include all that you need to do; write a done list of all the jobs you have completed. Not only does this help you reflect on how you've spent your time, it also allows you to celebrate and feel productive, which should translate into more productivity. You can decide to write this list daily or weekly, and when looking back at it in a month or a year you will feel a sense of pride.

AUTOMATE IT – USEFUL TECHNOLOGY

Technology has become one of the biggest distractions, but it also allows us to be more productive – from apps that allow us to network with people across the world, to software that allows us to schedule emails ahead of time, tech can be pretty useful. The trick here is to find tech that allows you to automate tasks and have less time playing in the apps.

Examples of what to automate and how

Emails: Gmail allows you to schedule emails and so does the software Boomerang.

Meetings: Calendly is a great way for creating an online calendar and allowing people to book time in with you. Doodle is also a great software to help find the best meeting time for people when you are working in groups.

Social media content: Schedule content online from tweets to Instagram Stories with apps like Planoly or Buffer.

BUILD HABITS

It's all good knowing the tasks that can make one productive, but what's more important is that they become habits which by virtue are automatic. We all have habits, whether we have been intentional about them or whether they have just grown on us. Habits can only come about once they are part of our routines and ingrained in our subconscious, which is strengthened by repetition. When we first start out in building a habit it will require a lot of effort but if we continue to repeat the action it will eventually lead to a habit. It has been said that it takes approximately 66 days for this to happen, but it can happen quicker if we connect our habit to a trigger point.

*

Finally, *be kind to yourself*. Running a side hustle is not easy simply because you have less time and more to do; the fact that you have started is something that should be celebrated. We won't all get this productivity thing right immediately but with time and dedication to working better these practices will become habits. We will learn to be focused on the important tasks that really make a difference.

GET TO WORK

1. Which areas of your productivity do you need to improve?
2. What steps do you need to take to improve those areas?
3. Use the OKR method to list out the goals you want to achieve with your side hustle for the next one year, six months and quarter. If you'd prefer to focus on shorter-term goals, only list what you will achieve for the next month.
4. Once you start working on your side hustle, begin to journal your feelings around your productivity. You can choose to do this at the end of each week, then based on your notes you can start to tweak which ways of working are doing well for you.
5. List the things that you spend your time on that are your biggest distractions to your side hustle. How can you minimise these distractions while working on your side hustle?

CASSANDRA STAVROU

Founder of PROPER Snacks

WHO IS CASSANDRA STAVROU?

Cassandra Stavrou is the founder of PROPER, makers of PROPERCORN and PROPERCHIPS. The biggest independent snack company in the UK, PROPER sells over five million bags per month and is stocked in 15 countries across Europe. Cassandra has become one of the leading voices in Europe for entrepreneurship, awarded an MBE in 2020 for services to the Food Industry and she sits on the UK Government's Food & Drink Council.

CASSANDRA'S STORY

For as long as I can remember, I've wanted to run my own business. Though my first ambition was to be an archaeologist, like Indiana Jones, I knew for certain from the age of 14 that I would end up working for myself. It took a serendipitous moment that put me on the path to PROPER.

I reluctantly studied law at university, then moved into advertising. It wasn't until I was 25 and working in Soho that I had the idea that changed everything. I saw the classic 3pm slump snack dash. The choice was something bland and unimaginative, which left you wanting more, or sugary and overindulgent, which left you feeling guilty. I wanted to create snacks where you didn't have to compromise. Popcorn was where I started.

I practically ran home to tell my mum about my idea. She reminded me that the last present my father bought me before he passed away when I was 16 was a vintage popcorn machine. It was an amazing bit of serendipity. It gave me the confidence to quit my job the next day and make PROPERCORN happen.

The truth is that even before then, running a business seemed more comfortable to me than working for someone else. I've always been fired up by the idea of turning a vision into reality. Building something from scratch and watching it solve a problem is the heart of entrepreneurship. That's how I get my kicks. I wasn't afraid of taking that step and I was prepared to take risks. That's the mentality you have to have if you're starting a business.

I had the idea to create PROPERCORN in 2009, and I hoped to crack it in a few months. Instead, it took a couple of years. The first year was undoubtedly the toughest. I was a young woman moving into a fiercely male industry and spent months traipsing up and down the country trying to convince a manufacturer to take me seriously. In the end, I was forced to make the first batches of popcorn in my mum's kitchen.

I needed to find a way to tumble the popcorn, so I refashioned a cement mixer. It was the best way to mix the corn with spices and ingredients. I needed to add oil, and on Top Gear they spoke about car paint spraying as the finest mist possible. I stole the idea, bought a kit and used that to mist the oil.

With PROPER, I was the target consumer. It meant when designing and creating the snacks and the brand I was able to make quick and intuitive decisions. I spent endless nights packing boxes and cold-calling potential customers before 2011, when things really got going.

Our first stockist was Google. A friend managed to get us a meeting with the head chef. They ordered 1,000 bags of PROPERCORN and it soon became the most popular snack out of the 48 they had on offer. Armed with that information, we went on to the big-name stockists and caught their attention. We now sell over five million bags per month.

To strike a deal with a big-name stockist, you have to have a great product, the right commercials (the business plan needs to stack up) but a bucket load of passion and determination as well. We were relentless in those early days and we never stopped. A decade on, that energy means we're front of the queue every time.

But having a clear vision of what you're trying to achieve is crucial, and I didn't just want to make popcorn. I wanted to use popcorn to provide a healthy alternative to a packet of crisps, raise the standards in our industry and build a company with a heart.

It had seemed so illogical that you had to compromise on taste and health when choosing snacks. And we had the perfect way to solve this problem. Everyone understands popcorn. There's something wonderfully nostalgic about it. I just wanted to make it properly and give it a new life.

There's a limit to how sure you can be that you'll be successful when you start a business. At some point, you need to just go for it. We're all armchair entrepreneurs, and those who have succeeded or even failed (those failures are just as important) are the ones who were brave enough to give it a go.

Mentorship was an important part to my journey at PROPER. In the early days, I was lucky to get some incredibly useful advice from Richard Reed, founder of Innocent Juice. But though mentorship is so important, it's vital that you really ask yourself what practical advice you need. And even then, mentorship should never come at the expense of learning on the job and figuring things out as you go along. Your naivety can be your secret weapon. It forces you to approach things in a fresh way.

Starting your own thing can be incredibly lonely. I regularly mentor other entrepreneurs, and we've often invited young start-ups to the PROPER offices to get support and desk space. I get my kicks from seeing talented people create something tangible from their ideas.

One really memorable challenge we had early on came about because we misunderstood the concept of shelf life. We thought we had six months to sell. We actually only had two. It could have bankrupted the business, but we were so determined to find a solution that we hit the phones, followed every lead, made hundreds of *cold calls – and we shifted all the stock. It generated huge momentum and kick-started our sales growth.*

In the early years of PROPER, *I was suffering with insecurities about being a woman in business and I was wasting time stewing over the wrong things. My mum eventually sat me down – as only mums can – and asked, 'Who do you think you are!?' She reminded me that people aren't going home dissecting everything you've done. They have their own stuff to deal with. People care a lot less than you think. I still find that by reminding myself of that, it can take the edge off.*

CASSANDRA'S WORDS OF WISDOM

- How does it make you feel? Human beings are creatures of emotion. That's how we make decisions. If it doesn't stir something within you, what meaning will it have with anyone else? In a world of increasing noise and distraction, find the confidence to back the ideas that stir you. Just because it seems logical doesn't guarantee success. The essential difference between emotion and reason is that emotion leads to action while reason leads to conclusions.

- Keep walking. We've always been restless, but it took a while for us to get confident with that. Changing your mind means you have one. An idea is never finished. Innovation never ends. And progress never comes from sitting still. So, remaining still may feel comfortable in that moment, but it'll leave you behind. It's restlessness and risk-taking that keeps you relevant.

- It's the company you keep. Anyone can write an exciting business plan. I did an average one 10 years ago. But if you don't have the team to make it happen, it is just an expensive dream. When I'm asked what I'm most proud of, I say the team. We recognised very quickly it's all about bringing in people better than you.

@cassandrastavrou
@Proper
proper.co.uk

2
TAKING OFF

The longest and probably the most important part of the book, this is where we determine whether your idea is something viable and worthy enough for you to start working on. We're going to save you time, effort and money – believe me when I say they are very easy to waste while in the process of figuring out this side-hustle journey. That being said, it's all part of the learning process, really, so no worries if you're already well on your way and have made many mistakes, at least you are ahead and have made significant progress.

HOW TO GET IDEAS

'Great ideas are nothing until they are executed.'

This is where you should have the most fun, let your mind travel far and wide and let your curiosity lead you. Great ideas are not exclusive. The goal here is that you are solution-focused and able to generate an idea that will provide a product or service that will solve the problem of your target audience. Also, remember that everyone can get ideas — this is just the beginning of the journey and you shouldn't stay here for too long. The next chapter will give you the advice you need to go beyond having ideas. For now, let's focus on how to generate them.

GIVE YOUR MIND SOME FRESH INSPIRATION

Ideas are not far away, they are very near and will likely come when you begin to get out in the world and try new things. It could start with the smallest of things, such as reading a different genre of book than your usual, listening to a new type of music, travelling to a new place to experience a new culture, or even mixing up your network to have new and varied types of conversations – this could be in real life via meet-ups or communities or on social media. I follow some of the most diverse minds on Twitter, LinkedIn and Instagram — people in different industries, with different interests in different locations – and this allows me to learn new things regularly, things I'd usually not come across. Our minds have a way of giving us the same old information when we continue to do the same old stuff and have the same old experiences, again and again — it's why I travel every quarter, to make sure I infuse myself with a new experience to birth new ideas. Fresh inspiration will bring fresh ideas when we step out of our usual lifestyle.

During a Masterclass session by Sara Blakely, founder of Spanx, she shared that she finds her best ideas when she is in the car, so she has created the habit of having 'a fake commute'. She wakes up an hour early to drive around town to get in her 'think time' when she can solve problems and when her best ideas come to her. After two years of not having a business name, she thought of the name Spanx while in her car.

So reflect on your experiences: where do you find the best ideas? For Albert Einstein, these came to him when he was shaving.

START WITH YOUR OWN EXPERIENCE

What problem are you experiencing that you could solve? Think about your everyday tasks, maybe the ones in your corporate job, as your own frustrations will help you to generate ideas. If you're focused on solving a problem that you personally face, you'll likely set out to make the best product or service possible. Many ideas have started this way: for example, for years Kim Kardashian has worn shapewear but has always struggled with finding ones that fit her well. She would cut up shapewear and sew pieces together so that it would fit her body correctly. She thought if she was finding it difficult to get shapewear that fits well, other women would be experiencing this too, so she decided to start her own line that would fit a variety of body shapes, called SKIMS.

USE YOUR EXPERTISE/ SKILL SET

What can you offer that everyone wants? Is it the expertise from your day job or a skill that you picked up over years of self-learning? One of my first businesses was a marketing and communications company for female founders; this was an expertise I already had and could offer as a service. How can you go a step further and do things differently? Could you create the ultimate guide, course or book – something that has the potential to scale? PR Dispatch, founded by Rosie Davies, is a PR subscription that gives small fashion brands access to her expertise in forms of press contacts, PR templates, pre-recorded lessons and support, all for £59 a month. She went from offering a service to creating a digital product, from being the services to creating a product, and now it's a business that can live without her.

THINK AHEAD

By keeping up with the news and current events, you are able to sense the type of problems that the world could face in the future or maybe how the usual things we do could start to change, such as an increase in flexible working and working from home which has made products like Zoom more relevant now than ever before. How can you start solving future problems now? Think ahead.

ASK OTHERS WHAT PROBLEMS THEY ARE FACING

There are problems everywhere and there are solutions waiting to be matched with them. An alternative to looking at your own problems is talking to others about what issues they would like solved. Ask friends, family, colleagues or even a niche audience such as writers, fashion designers, women in tech, etc., and stay empathetic towards the problems they are facing.

START WITH A PROBLEM NOT A SOLUTION

It's easy to think of *great* ideas and solutions, but this is working backwards. In this instance we must start from the beginning, which is with the problem, as this needs to exist in order for the idea to be relevant. This problem has to cause enough pain for people to search for a solution. Don't be limited by the fact that you are not personally experiencing this problem — as much as this may appear to be a weakness it is also a strength as your curiosity will lead you to question everything there is about the problem you are trying to solve. Some of the greatest brands are created by individuals who are not experiencing the problem they are solving. Your main goal is to identify the pain point of the target audience and provide a solution that will move them away from the pain and closer to what they desire.

For example, Heist is a direct-to-consumer brand that creates revolutionary underwear. The brand first started with tights but now make some of the best shapewear, bralettes and knickers out there – I have drooled over their Instagram page for so long and adored influencers who have marketed their product. How did they get it so right? Shapewear that doesn't make you feel like you are about to pass out and a brand that makes all types of women feel seen and included. I was so impressed by the brand that I decided to google the founder and, to my shock, discovered they are two men. They came up with the idea based on a conversation they had with their partners and decided they wanted to change an industry that lacked innovation and insight into how women experience underwear.

The Heist website reads: 'Through an innovative combination of technology from sports and space never before used in the category, and our scientific knowledge of the female form, we create underwear world-firsts that will change every woman's experience for good.' Firstly, they are knowledgeable about their audience, and secondly they are creating it like it's never been done before, through an innovative combination of technology taken from sports and science, which takes me to my next point.

Ideas do not need to create an aha moment, they won't always be unique — look at what currently exists and see how you can make it better or how you can reinvent the industry.

NOTHING IS NEW UNDER THE SUN

It's not about being the first, second or third to launch a particular product or service; to be quite honest, being the first does not mean you'll be the best. What you should be thinking is, how can I take my product or service and do things differently from 'the norm'? How can I solve the problem in a better way? How can I create such a brilliant solution that it causes people to switch from the status quo? How can I make a boring product fun? Monzo made banking cool and simple. Daye, a femcare brand, is using technology and CBD to solve women's health problems; they recently developed the 'world's first' CBD-infused tampon, to help soothe menstrual cramps. Their mission is to completely clean up the manufacturing process of tampons and make them much safer for women.

It doesn't have to be about product innovation but could be about how your brand speaks about a particular topic, how they manage their customer service. It's all about execution and adding your own 'sauce'.

Let's look at Frank Body, known for their cult coffee scrub. They are an Australian skincare brand with a full range of caffeinated products to support people in having soft and smooth skin. Apart from the fact that the product does what it says it will do, Frank Body stood out with strong visuals of coffee all over bodies, with captions such as 'unlike your ex, I'm non-toxic. I use natural and naturally derived ingredients.' No one had done it like this before and they managed it with no marketing budget. They are famously known for their witty way of talking, their coffee body pics and, of course, a product that works.

*

Jack Ellis, Pico co-founder, shared the below examples of companies that were created when similar brands existed:[9]

- Myspace (2003) – Facebook (2004)
- Yahoo! Mail (1997) – Gmail (2004)
- Basecamp (1999) – Asana (2008)
- Todoist (2007) – Wunderlist (2011)
- MSN Messenger (1999) – Skype (2003)
- Coca-Cola (1886) – Pepsi (1893)

Do not let the thought of someone saying your idea already exists put you off working on it, competition is healthy as it helps you think about how you can differentiate yourself.

LEAD WITH PASSION

Some of the best passion projects have become businesses, and whether or not they start out as such, I believe we should be passionate about the ideas we bring to life. I don't believe in working on ideas just to make money – the lack of passion is likely to lead to frustration when things are not going right.

---

[9] https://www.indiehackers.com/@pjrvs/why-are-you-building-x-when-y-exists -0edc3c5507

While important, it does not necessarily have to be passion about the market but it could be a passion about your mission or values – a bigger goal beyond a product or service.

WHAT OPPORTUNITIES SHOULD YOU FOCUS ON FOR THE NEAR FUTURE?

I spoke with two women who are in the business of looking out for the next trends and opportunities. These women spend their day-to-day jobs advising and investing in businesses, so knowing what will fly next is of high importance to them. Here is what they have to say:

Daisy Onubogu, Head of Network, BACKED VC
- Community. Still a trend, but different from the first iteration we experienced, which was more marketing-focused: loose associations to drive brand affinity, rather than an effort to create real relationship bonds between people. Now I think we'll see businesses offering the experience of a genuine community as a product in and of itself. For instance, we started with coworking spaces with brand-association-labelled community, now there are things such as work near home spaces, community hubs where the service offering is the creation of real ties between you and others in your neighbourhood/area – these will likely be good for communal towns. Whether something as human and critical as a community *should* be commoditised is still debatable: if you have to pay to get into these communities then who gets let in and who gets left out? If the main

pursuit of companies is profit, what critical elements of community creation will they compromise on?

- Healthcare industry. Our fears around diseases, and antibiotic resistance in general, are on the rise and if we take the situation we are in now with a pandemic, I believe because of this we will see quite a lot of funding going towards it and an increase in consumer appetite for products and services that prevent ill health. This was previously an uncool space for VC investment, given consumer apathy and complexities of selling into healthcare stakeholders like the NHS, but has now become attractive to funders who recognise the commercial opportunity.

Anna Turner, Insight Director, Ogilvy

- Sustainability. Awareness of and interest in sustainability has reached a tipping point in the last year. The climate crisis can no longer be ignored and it's driving people to think more about the way they live, the way they consume things and the impact they are having on the world around them. People are becoming more conscious as consumers – conscious of what they are buying, of how it's been produced, what they are wasting and the impact that has on the environment. People are embracing social causes and are increasingly expecting products, brands and companies to put purpose before profits, to genuinely stand for something and give back and make a positive contribution to their surroundings. Within the food industry, there is increased awareness and interest in food waste in terms of cost and impact on the environment, food security, exploitation of land and labour, long-term sustainability, local sourcing and the general impact of food production on the environment. And in terms of the fashion industry, sustainable fashion is becoming more mainstream. People are increasingly interested in ethical production, the environmental impact and footprints of materials and the production methods of the clothes they are buying, as well as waste, prompting the rising interest in the circular fashion economy.

- Technology has underpinned fundamental changes in every aspect of our life in 2020 and has impacted everyone regardless of age or previous level of tech literacy. The speed of change has been so rapid that the shift experienced in technology becoming mainstream over the course of 2020 is something that would have typically taken 5–10 years to achieve in ordinary times and there's no going back now. New apps, technology platforms, VR and AI technologies have meant that people have been able to stay connected with others virtually when real-life interaction is not possible. It has also enabled a mass rollout of remote learning/education, made virtual entertainment and livestreaming mainstream and ensured that exercise and fitness have seamlessly transitioned online. There was already a big shift to e-commerce before the pandemic struck, but without physical stores altogether, digital commerce has been reimagined, with companies incorporating elements of the physical shopping experience to the online experience using technologies like VR and AI.

As I mentioned earlier, this is just the beginning of the journey; ideas are a dime a dozen and are not set in stone. Your idea will likely evolve over time while you start to gain more information about your customer through research or find out more about the market or industry. On that note, don't get hung up with the idea, just get started, because execution wins over ideas.

If you've thought up a few ideas by now and are wondering which ones to choose, try some of these below.

Things to consider when selecting an idea

- The one you just can't seem to get out of your mind.
- The time it will cost you.
- The idea that makes something easier that was once difficult.
- The solution to a problem that you understand and experience.
- A product that already has a market and a demand (how much demand is debatable!).
- A project in which you have previous experience and are the most suitable person to launch – this is what they call founder market fit.
- Do you have the money?
- The idea that gives you a sense of purpose or mission in life.

NAYSAYERS

There will be people who will try to put you off from investing time in your idea; family and friends who all want to shield you – those close to you will want to protect you from failing. Consider when it's best to share your news with people that you know. The opinions that you should care about are those of people who will help you move your business forward. Tell them, but make sure these people sign non-disclosure agreements to protect yourself.

This quote by American businesswoman Mary Kay is one that I want to leave you with: 'Ideas are a dime a dozen, it's the people that implement them that are priceless.' We all have million-dollar ideas but very few of us will take action to make them happen, so get ready to take action.

GET TO WORK

1. List all your ideas that come to mind.
2. Shortlist two to three ideas using the information in this chapter.
3. Go through the three ideas and decide which is the biggest problem you are facing that needs to be solved to make your business a success.
4. Think of three or four existing products or services in your industry that look the same and figure out how you could do something different.
5. Could you do this idea on your own? If not, what would you need or who would you need to get started?

UNSAH MALIK

Author, Social Media Expert & Founder of The Modern Go-getter

WHO IS UNSAH MALIK?

Unsah Malik is a social media expert who launched the topselling ebook Slashed It, which led to the start of her journey to entrepreneurship and she founded The Modern Go-getter, an online publication modernising entrepreneurship. Unsah started her career in digital at the age of 17, making sure that she had a wealth of knowledge and experience before graduating from university, putting her steps ahead of her peers and on the path to becoming an expert in the business.

UNSAH MALIK'S STORY

I am not a born entrepreneur; I never had the entrepreneurial ambition within me to have my own business. What I did have, though, was the fire within me to always want to be 100 per cent the best at whatever I work on, regardless of the role I found myself in. Luckily, from young, I knew what I wanted to focus my professional career on: being a journalist and working for glossy magazines or newspapers. Knowing this gave me a head start, so I started interning from about 17 years old. I bombarded editors, local newspapers, bloggers who no one had heard of and pleaded with them to allow me to write for them, even if it was not paid – I was living at home at the time so working for free was okay.

In the early 2000s the social media boom took place. I became interested and decided this was something I wanted to understand and become the best at. I started off by teaching myself about it. I saw publications and brands starting to use social media and spent time observing and learning the skills needed to excel in the industry. During university I started to pitch again to editors but this time I started to include social media management support. At this point companies were not too concerned about social media so they handed the control over to me. By the time I was in my second year of university I had a wealth of experience, but I decided to still take a gap year out to do another whole year of interning in an established editorial team where I could learn from someone. The company I went with was the start-up, Suitcase Magazine, founded by Serena Guen.

I was hired full-time and became the assistant digital editor. Serena encouraged me to take control of the social media as she could see the desire I had for it — I really appreciated this about Serena and it is so important that we surround ourselves with people that push us forward in our careers. I continued in this role and became an expert while I was completing my third year at university. During this time I won a digital writing competition with Elle magazine on the news desk, where I was the social media manager, and then E! Entertainment brought me on board for a community management job. They had assumed I was an experienced graduate, not knowing I was still a student, which proved how well I knew my job and how much experience I had picked up for myself. I went on to finish the third year but, to my shock, I pretty much knew more than the lecturers at one point because I had spent so long working on the job. After graduating I worked for the Guardian and worked my way up through different roles and focused simply on social media.

I started working for a luxury beauty brand, Rodial Beauty, and discovered influencer marketing. In this influencer marketing role, I grew very fast and built a black book of contacts. Influencer marketing is about humans, so it's important to be an excellent communicator and when there is not a huge amount of budget you have to work above and beyond in nurturing those relationships. It was during this time that I started to offer people advice for free. I never minded I was giving it away for free. I just wanted to educate bloggers, who we now know as influencers, how brands worked, as it was still very early and they had no idea how to navigate relationships and deals with brands. At the back of my mind, I started to wonder if I could become a consultant. I was receiving feedback that I would be great at it, but I was so keen on getting that strong experience and really becoming an expert in my niche. Looking back at it now, that is the best decision I had made. I could have left my role at Suitcase and gone on to be a consultant but all the experience after that has made me the expert that I am today.

After working at Rodial I had gained a lot of influencer and social media experience, I was constantly being asked questions on social so I decided to create a post: '10 ways to increase your engagement'. It went viral, and from this I decided to start uploading my advice onto social media, specifically Instagram, Twitter and LinkedIn. This was a passion and I had no intention to turn it into a business. I genuinely liked sharing the knowledge I had in my niche to help people out.

After a while, when the account had grown to 4,000 followers, I decided to write a book. I wrote the ebook as I was being asked too many questions and had no time to answer everyone individually — an ebook would allow people to get answers instantly and have access to my knowledge. The first step I took was to write the contents page and a few sentences, then I took a picture and uploaded this to Instagram announcing I was writing a book – when I get an idea, I don't wait. It took me seven or eight months to write this book. I teach people from different angles such as understanding your niche, the different types of social media, how to increase engagement. Posting that image on social media was soft marketing for me which led to me receiving the same question often: 'When is your book coming out?' By the time my ebook was ready to launch, I had a strong database of people who believed in my expertise. This is all I know, and this is why it is my area of expertise.

I put the ebook out in July and I hit five figures in sales. The famous story everyone likes to repeat is 'Unsah made £15,000 *from her ebook in 5 hours,' but they forget I'm here because of my years of expertise.*

I started building this audience and page while in my 9–5 and I was very transparent with my employer about this. *In previous roles I had to hide what I was doing. We can't expect every employer to appreciate that we have other interests outside of our role. My employer was very supportive, and I had to adjust into my new role whilst also writing, but because it was my niche I knew what I was doing. It took time but it was not hard to do.*

During the pandemic, *I was furloughed but kept continuing to grow my social media presence based on the content I was sharing. I decided to launch the ebook and with its success, a week or two after this, I decided to leave my role and focus on growing this brand and turning it into a business.*

The best thing about using your skill as your niche *is that because you've been in the market for so long, you already have a decent idea of everything that's going on. I wasn't infiltrating my way into something new. I was making a bigger name for myself in the only world I knew. I graduated and worked as a journalist, so I had been writing for a long time — and then my title was always Digital or Social Media-something. The ebook is a combination of both ... nothing less and nothing more.*

The answers I needed before I wrote my ebook *came to me before I even decided to write it, through all the problems others came to* me for while I was working away throughout the years. But I still needed to check how high the demand was, what other people found attractive from people in the same market as me, and the price people were willing to pay. There's no point putting in effort for something with little evidence of you being able to monetise it. Ironically, I found that the general audience were paying a little too much for advice from charlatans, and what people found attractive also happened to be what 10 times more people found unattractive. So, that became both my initial appeal — the 'no-BS' tone — and my competitive advantage. To others, it was like, 'Here's someone with this many years of experience who's worked for some big names in-house, and look, she's not charging thousands for basic information and facts like "how to pick a hashtag" or "you should use video content" ... and look, she's even giving away so much for free on her social channels.'

Before writing a full ebook, I launched a free mini ebook, and while it definitely served the initial purpose as value to the potential customer, it was also additional research for myself. You could say I dipped my toes in before swimming the lengths. Okay, people wanted me to share my knowledge, but would they read pages and pages' worth? Would they instantly download it? Would they leave me a review? Would they be even more excited for the version I'll make them pay for?

In many ways, I still research — I research my audiences heavily. It's where 70 per cent of my efforts go, if not more. I'm not bothered about naysayers and external noise. I'm not too bothered about competition either. I only care about my audience, what they want, and what people similar to my followers would also want.

UNSAH'S WORDS OF WISDOM

- Create valuable content from the get-go for free: The biggest mistake people make is waiting until their product or service is ready to launch before creating content and going full steam on social media. Show people you're different by exploring topics within your niche and adding your USP for a competitive advantage. Allow people the chance to be curious about you and understand your worth in the market. The money will flow far easier once people really believe in you — and if you time it right, enough people will by the time you're ready to present a product or service they should pay for.

- Build a community by capitalising on two-way interaction: The beauty of social media is that you can build a rapport with your followers and customers better than any other medium has allowed. The only way you're going to build a community as a newbie is by interacting with others, engaging in meaningful conversations, asking for their opinions and valuing the time they spend speaking to you.

- Niche down as much as possible: Avoid being a jack-of-all-trades. It will only confuse people over what you're about and what you can do for them — and confusion is a huge deterrent. Become a person that others want to go to for a very specific topic or need. Once you've grown more of a following, you can expand into different areas (this is what I call 'sub-niches').

@unsahmalik
slashedit.co.uk

HOW'S IT GONNA MAKE MONEY?

'If it doesn't make you money, then it's most probably an expensive hobby.'

You need to start thinking about how you are going to make profit from your idea, how you plan to charge your customers and how you intend to market your product — this is what is referred to as a business model.

One of the important factors for any business that wants to survive long term is achieving a positive cash flow – basically, having enough cash to pay bills and keep the business running while making a profit. A successful business model needs to have more money coming in than it does going out – this is profit – and without this things can become a struggle and unsustainable.

The model you decide to go with depends on the nature of your idea, but most importantly on the needs of your customers.

WHY YOUR BUSINESS MODEL MATTERS

Knowing about these business models isn't just for you to pick one and say, 'Here is how we will make money,' but to also understand what your industry has been known to use and how you can change the industry by bringing in a new business model.

Dollar Shave Club is a razor-blade brand offering one-dollar subscriptions on blades. Typically, this industry sold mainly through retailer to consumer, but now there is a direct to consumer and subscription service which has changed how things are being done. With this model, Dollar Shave Club are able to retain customers easily as they have direct access to them while also offering them convenience.

TYPES OF MODELS

Here is a brief summary of business models that you could use for your idea, but also take note that you can create a new model that would work effectively for your customers. The needs of your customer is what dictates your business model.

ADVERTISING-BASED MODEL

This type of model is where the business makes profit by advertising products or services to a large audience. This tends to be a business that is focused on creating content for people, which can vary from podcasting and videos to games or articles. Your customers are both the advertiser and your viewers. Although advertisers are normally focused on reaching large audiences, they are now working with businesses that have smaller, more niche ones and are looking more into engagement than audience size.

Example: Blavity Inc is a media company founded by Morgan Debaun. The company produces digital media content for Black millennials and generates money through ads on their website and through brand partnerships. Another example is a games app in which customers play for free but the company makes money through the adverts that they show (those annoying little pop-ups, you know them!).

This model is great if you are able to consistently churn out good-quality content and drive engagement.

SUBSCRIPTION MODEL

If you are looking for consistent recurring revenue, this is the model for you. The subscription model typically tends to charge a monthly or annual fee for a product or service, ranging from makeup to food or clothes. Below are two types of subscriptions.

The curation model

As the name suggests, this subscription includes a curation of products in every delivery, giving the receiver something new and fresh to look forward to. This does mean you'd need to have something new available every month or however often you send out a subscription package, which can be time-consuming to manage; however, due to the nature of the model you'll have consistent income and can prepare for inventory.

Example: UK-based entrepreneur Jamelia Donaldson, who previously ran TreasureTress as a side hustle, offers a personalised monthly subscription box of specially handpicked natural hair products and beauty treats for young black women and girls. TreasureTress works with brands such as Pantene, Shea

Moisture, TRESemmé and Cantu. She has kept the team lean with six employees and ships to over 26 countries.

The access model

This model provides exclusivity to subscribers by offering them access to services and products that only paying subscribers can view, while in some cases restricting non-paying subscribers to limited access.

Example: Femstreet, founded by Sarah Nöckel, is a monthly subscription newsletter offering access to a slack community, premium content and talks focused on women in tech and venture capital. Sarah, who runs this membership community alongside her role as venture capitalist, has grown the community to over 500 subscribers. Her non-paying subscribers receive the newsletter but do not have access to the exclusive community and content.

FREEMIUM MODEL

This model allows customers to utilise some basic services for free but, if they want more, they have to upgrade to the paid version. This model has been said to help quicken recurring revenue compared to a paid-only model as the basic free services lure customers in.

Example: The Bumble app used for dating, finding friends and creating business connections allows you to use the app with limited features. If you upgrade your profile then you have access to the full features of the app. Another great example is LinkedIn which allows you to showcase your work experience for free but paying members have access to additional features, including being able to reach out to people who they are not connected with and also to view analytics covering whether a recruiter has visited their page or how a job application is performing.

DIRECT-TO-CONSUMER MODEL (D2C)

With this model you cut out the middle man in the process such as retailers and sell directly to your customer, making profit from your sales transactions. Some say this model is harder as you have to look for customers yourself, but I honestly believe it allows you to build a better one-on-one relationship with your customer, allowing for them to become loyal and to later develop into a community.

It goes without saying that you as the founder will have complete control over your brand, reputation, marketing and sales tactics — something some retailers tend to mess up.

Example: Glossier, founded by Emily Weiss back in 2014 off the back of her beauty blog called 'Into the Gloss', is a beauty brand that serves customers directly. Emily has been able to differentiate her brand by building a strong community of followers through content and experiences. I remember being in New York in 2019 and deciding to visit the Glossier HQ — the queue of women (some including their partners: see @glossierboyfriends) went round the corner of the street, sales assistants were clothed in all-pink jumpsuits and greeted you with huge smiles. I entered and was wowed by the setup, young girls rushed in and took off their coats, screaming 'OMG we're in Glossier'. I was in awe of the obsession but quickly realised this is what it means to build a community — it's admirable, and it is hard, but you can start somewhere.

Another example is Away luggage, the brilliant brand that is changing the face of travel, who have displayed on their website their business model to their consumers for transparency's sake and why this business model serves the customer better.

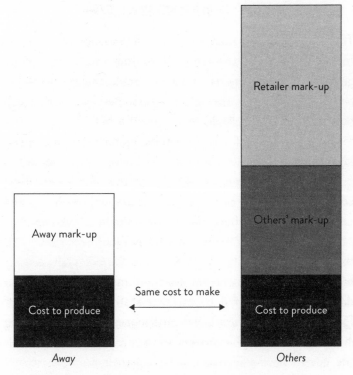

Example of Direct-to-Consumer model for Away luggage brand[10]

---

[10] https://www.awaytravel.com/uk/en/our-story

This business model is likely to be your method when you are starting out; however, it is becoming more and more popular and harder to get noticed — as Neil Blumenthal, CEO of designer eyewear brand Warby Parker noted in the *New York Times*, 'It's never been cheaper to start a business, although I think it's never been harder to scale a business.'

RETAIL MODEL

This is a traditional model that is the opposite of the D2C model, as here you use retailers (typically brick and mortar stores) and resellers to help take your business into the market and sell to your customers – they buy from you on a large scale and sell on the products.

Example: MDMflow is a cosmetic brand founded by Florence Adepoju and launched in 2013 after she spent her undergrad years working in luxury retail. Florence, who is a cosmetic scientist, made her own lipsticks for women of colour. The cosmetic brand sold in stores like Topshop, Nasty Gal, Harvey Nichols and Boots, which helped her go from making 30 lipsticks a day to 300. With Lena Dunham showcasing MDMflow on her Instagram, this took Florence up to 900 a day and sales were flying in from Harvey Nichols and Look Fantastic. However, one of the challenges Florence noted that she experienced in this process was late payments from retailers, despite having payment terms in place.

Retail is a great platform but it is now incredibly hard to get your brand into the big retailers and there can be a delay in getting paid for your products.

MARKETPLACE MODEL

A marketplace is a platform that allows people to make transactions between themselves, which could be monetary or value-based. Marketplaces can be business to business (B2B), business to customer (B2C) or peer to peer.

Example: Beauty Stack, founded by Sharmadean Reid, economically empowers women by helping them sell their beauty and wellness services in a social marketplace. Beauty professionals post images of their work on the app and potential clients can book directly from an image, see what their friends are booking and like and save their favourite treatments.

Platforms with this model would usually make money via charging a listing fee, a subscription or maybe even taking a commission from every sale made through the app.

RENTING MODEL

This model is as straightforward as the name: it is when the customers come to a platform to rent a product that has been listed either by the businesses or via a marketplace.

- One-off renting model: Here customers would make a one-off payment to rent an item and maybe pay an extra amount for delivery.
- Renting subscription model: This is where you must pay a subscription fee to the platform before you can rent.

There is also the option to combine both models.

Example: Feather is a New York City-based furniture rental subscription service that offers both models at once. As mentioned in an Inc interview with the founder: 'Feather members pay a monthly $19 subscription fee plus the cost to rent each individual item. For instance, a living-room package that includes a sofa, lounge chair, coffee table, and floor lamp will set you back $90 to $167 a month. Members can swap out items for free once a year, depending on their changing needs or tastes. Subsequent swaps will trigger a $99 delivery fee. Non-members can also rent from Feather, though they pay a $99 delivery fee each time and higher per-item fees. A Deco Weave West Elm 'Eddy' sofa that runs $39 a month for members costs $134 a month for non-members.'

ENTERPRISE MODEL

This is a company that sells its service or software to another organisation on a licence or contract. The term of the licence/contract would be fixed and then renewed at the end of that period.

*

So when developing your side hustle, the model you decide to go with depends on the nature of your idea but most importantly on the needs of your customers. As we've seen with some examples above, you can have hybrid business models, so get creative in thinking about how you can sell your products and generate revenue.

IS YOUR BUSINESS MODEL SCALABLE?

When thinking of your idea, always have at the back of your mind, 'Can this be scaled?' This was advice that a mentor once gave me. To scale means to create substantial growth without crashing, which used to be quite challenging for many service-based businesses such as coaches and personal trainers as they used to only offer 1:1 services, but now many are offering group coaching/group training or online courses, which can give the same or similar results and allows them the opportunity to scale.

*

In order to stay relevant, you should often revisit your business model to see if there is room for innovation — Netflix's business model was able to wipe out the popular Blockbuster video rental chain that filed for bankruptcy in 2010 and closed all remaining stores in 2013.[11] As I write this book during the height of the 2020 global pandemic, I have seen several small

[11] Johnson, M.W. (2018). *Reinvent Your Business Model: How to Seize the White Space for Transformative Growth.*

and large businesses having to pivot and revisit their business model – from Airbnb who started offering online experiences, to the Instagram chef who started offering an online group cookery course, there is a need to adapt when the environment calls for it. That being said we shouldn't wait for times to get 'bad', every business should consider change as it develops and becomes more successful.[12]

PRICING

Asides from picking a model that will help you build a sustainable business, how do you decide how much you charge? A starting point is to charge more than what it costs to create your product or service and to add what it takes to keep the business running, including what you'd like to also pay yourself — this model will not work for every business but it is a good starting point.

How much you eventually decide to charge is down to you. Outside the cost of making the product, how much do you feel it's worth? Are you scared to charge a higher price? Money is the oxygen for your side hustle to survive. While it's okay to initially put your own money into your side hustle to get it off the ground, it should eventually be able to fund itself and that can only happen once you start charging accordingly.

---

[12] www.inc.com/sean-wise/ikea-is-testing-a-44-billion-pivot-to-its-business-model
-heres-why-its-a-brilliant-strategy.html?cid=search

THINGS TO CONSIDER

- In the next chapter, we will discuss how to create customer profiles. Consider how you can have a range of different-priced products for your varying types of customers — think tiered pricing.
- Price based on how often your customer will be buying from you, such as cost of buying tampons vs the cost of a one-off online course. The latter is likely to be bought once a year and you can decide to charge at a premium price whereas tampons are likely to be bought every month so it needs to be a price that someone can be comfortable spending on a regular basis.
- Price the product based on how much your customer thinks it's worth – perception is reality.

GET TO WORK

1. Make a list of businesses that exist in your industry and highlight the ones that have interesting business models. Can you combine some models to give you a better advantage?
2. List all the ways your business can generate revenue.
3. How much will you charge for your product? What are all the extra costs you need to add on top?

EMMA GANNON

Author and Podcaster

WHO IS EMMA GANNON?

Emma Gannon is a Sunday Times *bestselling author, speaker, novelist and host of the number one careers podcast in the UK, 'Ctrl Alt Delete'. She began her career working in digital media agencies, then Bauer Media, Condé Nast, and has since been published in places like the* Telegraph, the Guardian, Vanity Fair and Elle, *as well as being a columnist for the* Telegraph, COURIER *and the* Sunday Times.

She also writes a weekly newsletter called The Hyphen that is an exploration of ideas that have got her thinking in new ways, and an online book club, The Hyphen Book Club.

EMMA'S STORY

I published my first book with Penguin in 2016, called Ctrl Alt Delete: How I Grew Up Online, *which documented my own stories of young millennial life on the internet, from cyber bullying to friendship to dating. When the book came out, I had just written a lot of words about myself and I didn't want to talk about myself any* more! However, I wasn't done talking about the subject of 'life online', so I decided to interview other people instead and create a podcast to share their stories. So the 'Ctrl Alt Delete' podcast was born in April 2016, and I interviewed a wide range of guests about what the internet means to them. I was lucky enough to use some of the contacts I'd made through my day job at Glamour magazine, or friends I'd made on Twitter, to secure the first few guests. The podcast has evolved over time and now it's mostly about creative careers, mental health and how the internet obviously plays a huge part in all of our lives. I've just published my 300th episode, and I still love making it.

I didn't really have any plans growing up. The careers advice was quite stunted — which led me to write my book The Multi-Hyphen Method. I am quite an open-minded person, and so I always knew I'd probably be going with the flow of whatever life threw at me. My career is basically a zig-zag instead of a straight line. My dad quit his job and became self-employed in his forties and it changed his life, so I think subconsciously I had an early positive influence on seeing the benefits and freedom of self-employment, which I definitely acknowledge as a huge privilege.

Even though it was only four and a half years ago, podcasting wasn't really the big industry it is now, and people were not building careers or businesses off the back of this industry. So I just got to try it out without anyone looking really. My friends and family don't work in the media space so they didn't really listen or look at what I was doing, but my friends in the blogging/magazine industry and my first listeners were really supportive, and I got really positive feedback straight away (even though I had a lot to learn in terms of audio!). It's important to note that I did not know it would *work when I started, nor did I expect to make money from it. I thought of it as a 'trial' that I'd do for fun on the side of my job, to market the book, and then take it from there. I think it's really important not to put really high expectations on yourself. If I'd sat down and said: 'Right, today I'm going to launch an award-winning podcast,' I would never have started it.*

Over the years, a lot of opportunities have come about to start a business because of the internet. *Here is a glimpse of the business model I use for my own business: I have hosted adverts at the beginning of each episode, and I occasionally partner with brands I like on branded episodes. It seems most people like listening to podcasts for free, and therefore don't mind listening to the occasional advert in exchange for a rich 40-minute piece of content. I usually collaborate with technology and lifestyle brands, and I only partner with brands I like or would use myself. I am also the author of four books and have regular speaking engagements.*

I am proud of the steady growth of the podcast, and I'm glad I didn't use any 'hacks' to grow it faster. *I don't believe in cutting corners, and I am a big fan of doing things the long-term, organic way and building a proper audience over time. If I'd known it was going to turn into the successful business it is now I probably would have invested in some better microphones at the start!*

EMMA'S WORDS OF WISDOM

- Other people don't really 'know better'; if I had realised this from the beginning, I would have listened to less advice and just followed my gut.

- Getting your hands dirty and trying things out is always a better way of spending your time than just endlessly listening to other people's advice. You can't copy and paste someone else's path so you might as well try things out your own way.

@emmagannon
emmagannon.co.uk

DO YOUR HOMEWORK: MARKET AND USER RESEARCH

'Be obsessed with your customer more than your competitor.'

As much as I would like to say 'just do it' once you've landed on your idea, it would be silly for me to suggest that you immediately jump from idea to working on the solution without conducting any research. It's through the research that you save time, money and quickly learn what will work and what won't – don't be fooled by what your friends and family have said about your idea, the question is: would they buy it?!

I was scrolling through Instagram one day and saw a budding entrepreneur sharing her mistakes, a few that I was surprised to hear — she wasn't the first to start the type of business she was running but it was obvious that she hadn't done her research, based on the pitfalls she was experiencing. I reached out to her and asked her to read a particular article that she might find useful, one where a founder had shared all the mistakes she had made. Mistakes are great lessons in disguise, but if they can be avoided at all costs, why not? We don't all have to fail to learn, we can learn from others or learn through research by understanding the market we are entering, our customers and competitors.

Time is your most valuable resource — don't waste it on something that you don't even know is going to work.

This chapter will cover how to go about conducting research, to save you time, money and effort on this journey of side hustling.

Just a heads up that this is most likely not the most fun chapter, but it is the most important in order for you to create a sustainable and profitable side hustle. Research is easy to overlook if you get carried away with the excitement, but it will save you from a business that only has the reality of surviving a short couple of years.

VALIDATING YOUR IDEA

Now that you have your idea, to clear any doubts you may have about it, there are two phases that you will go through to help you validate it, to see if your idea really needs to exist and to learn more about your customers: 1) market and user research; 2) running experiments. These two phases will help you determine if there is enough interest in your idea and feedback on the next steps you need to take, whether you need to pivot or if you should carry on building your business as you were.

We aren't looking for perfection here, we are trying to see what needs to stay and what needs to go. Don't be too hard on yourself if your customers say what you created is absolutely pants – okay, what do you do to make it better? Reframe your thinking. Turn your problems or feedback into opportunities. Business is an experiment and if we all approach it like this then we will lead with curiosity and will be open to making changes if and when necessary.

The information will also shed some light on the interests of your customers and allow you to build out customer profiles and determine what marketing messages will work best for your product or service.

Validating your idea will not only help you select your best idea but will also give you the confidence you need to launch and, if you decide to, to make it your main hustle.

When I started For Working Ladies, it began as a digital content site – aka a blog, as some would call it. Before it launched, I had reached out to 20–30 women on LinkedIn who had writer, journalist or communications in their bio and asked them if they'd be interested in writing for a new media site I was launching for women. To my shock (still shocked today) the majority of them said yes. There was no website in place and neither did they know who I was BUT they all wanted a site like this to exist. So when the website launched I had 20–30 articles pre-written and went on to edit them myself.

For me, the response from the writers was the validation that I needed to get started. I had also spoken to friends and started an Instagram account where I was posting content around the interests of my audience and was getting good engagement. Once we started to market the content, we were getting 10,000–20,000 website hits a month. It's not a lot, I know, but for someone who was just sharing content in Facebook groups, I think it did pretty well. One thing I wish I did was understand how a digital media publication works, because I was really winging it at this stage and I've now gone on to change a lot of things.

In startup expert Eric Ries' book *The Lean Startup* it suggests that we ask ourselves these questions when building our idea:

- Do consumers recognise that they have the problem you are trying to solve?
- If there was a solution, would they buy it?
- Would they buy it from you?
- Can we build a solution for that problem?

Sometimes your customer is not aware that they are facing the problem you are trying to solve, so this is an opportunity for you to bring this to light – they could have the pain point and not know why. For example, many women have experienced severe problems with their menstrual cycle, not knowing this may be due to the use of mass-made sanitary towels that are filled with toxins — Ohne, the natural period products company, has made it their mission to educate women on this and provide ethical alternatives. During the user research stage, it would be important to highlight this information, present a solution and ask if they would buy your product if it existed.

Doing the research and experimenting will help you to gather information on three things:

1. The industry.
2. The competition: collect information about them, analyse the most common problems and try to address one or all of them. Also decide how you can offer something different.
3. Your customers: patterns, characteristics, spending habits and influences.

RESEARCH

When it comes to research, both market research and user research are important. They are carried out at different stages of creating a product and both use data to inform their decisions. The type of research you need to do depends on the *questions* you want to answer and the kind of *information* you need to support your idea.

Market research gives broad information about customers, competition and the industry — it may not be clear or specific about what customers *really* want, but this can help you to develop your business model or plan. User research is much more valuable as it gives deep insights into what the customer pain points are and helps to give you an understanding of customer behaviour and have empathy towards the customer.

Market research vs user research	
Market research	**User research**
Broad overview	Deep insights
Attitudes to products	Consumer behaviours
Informs marketing decisions	Informs design decisions
Insight into what people buy	Insight into how people choose a product
Covers a broad spectrum of consumers	Covers a smaller quantity of consumers
Determines quantity of product needed	Decides quality of product

METHODS FOR CONDUCTING MARKET RESEARCH

Essentially, the more you know about your market and your consumers, the better for your business. Here are a few great starting points to help you uncover that useful knowledge.

Internet

From social media to Google, there is a vast amount of information that you can find online about the market and your competitors, including:

- Euromonitor
- CB Insights
- Mintel

- eMarketer
- PWC Research & insights
- Euromonitor
- Statista
- www.business-live.co.uk
- startups.co.uk

Library

In the business section you will find reports, journals or online databases that you can access to support your research.

Trade publications

Trade publications will share insights around how the industry is performing, current trends and also competitor information that can help your research. Examples include *Vogue Business, Business of Fashion* and *Campaign*.

Interviewing experts

Experts in the industry will have a wealth of knowledge about things to avoid and what to look out for – they can also double up as mentors, if you're lucky.

Reviews

Reviews on competitors can give you an insight into how they are performing and what problems they are solving – effectively or not.

Engaging with competitors at
different touch points

Engage via social media, email, website, pop-up and retail with other brands, so you can experience what they are like.

Sales assistants in stores

If the product is in store, asking sales assistants how the brand is performing or how customers engage with the product can provide you with useful information.

METHODS FOR CONDUCTING
USER RESEARCH

Below are some effective methods for conducting user research.

User surveys

This is a popular approach as it is the simplest to do and if done well it can be a brilliant tool.

Self-serving platforms to help you run surveys:

- Google Forms
- SurveyMonkey
- Typeform

Platforms that you can pay to help you with building and executing your surveys:

- IdeaCheck.io
- Attest (Askattest.com)
- Tectonic

Focus groups

These are interviews with small groups of people from similar demographics which will help you to understand their ideas, opinions and beliefs about the competitor's product/service/industry and see their reactions to certain questions. You should try to make this experience as informal as possible; perhaps don't call this a focus group, try something interesting that would make them feel like they belong to a special group, for example, call them 'the inner circle'.

Customer interviews

One-on-one interviews — this is a success when the interview questions and techniques have been carefully designed with well-thought-out questions.

Observation

Depending on the product or service, observing your customers can give insight into how a product should be made. For example, if you are creating a printer to sell specifically to retail shops, it would be useful to observe how they use this in the shops in conjunction with other tasks to really hone in on their day-to-day requirements – this can then help them when looking at including additional features for the printer.

Asking customers to trial competitors' products/services

If you are moving into a very popular industry, it's great to focus on what your competitors are getting wrong by asking your potential customers where they see the gaps are or assessing their behaviour when using the product or service. You can decide to remove the branding of the products/services when customers are interacting with them so there are no biases.

COMPETITION

When starting a business you must understand where the other players operate, to help you decide how you will be better and different than what is out there already. These are the things that will help your potential customer determine whether to switch over to your product/service.

The type of questions you should consider finding information on:

- Who are your competitors?
- How long have they existed?
- Where are they located?
- What resources do they have access to?
- Who is their target market?
- What are their prices?
- What are their strengths and weaknesses?
- How do they communicate and market their brand?
- Are they funded?

KEEP IT SIMPLE

In the beginning you may not be able to part ways with your cash to give it to research gurus and the like, so my advice is to get creative on how you can carry out research in a budget-friendly way. Google is your friend and there are several communities that could help you with focus groups.

MAKE NO ASSUMPTIONS

Business Insider reported that an influencer, @Arii on Instagram, whose real name is Arianna Renee, decided to launch her own clothing line, ERA, with an initial drop of T-shirts. She had 2.6 million followers yet she failed to sell 36 T-shirts, having assumed that her huge following would translate to sales.[13] In an Instagram post she shared that she had poured her heart into the brand, flew a photographer and makeup artist over, was lucky enough to gather some friends to model for her and lastly rented a photo studio for video and photo promo. She went on to share that she had been receiving really good feedback and was convinced people were going to buy her clothing. The influencer said she had been told by the company producing the brand that she needed to sell at least 36 T-shirts from the first run of products in order for the line to be continued, but Renee didn't hit the target.

---

[13] https://www.insider.com/instagrammer-arii-2-million-followers-cannot-sell-36-t-shirts-2019-5#:~:text=An%20Instagram%20star%20has%20sparked, initial%20drop%20of%20T%2Dshirts.

Influencer marketing expert Shirley Leigh-Wood Oakes explained, 'It's far too simplistic to assume followers will equate to customers — you need to know your potential consumers. Some influencers know their followers and what they want from the influencer. Whether it's their fashion style or their beauty advice, they review what their followers go for and they market to that.'

There were so many things that went wrong with this influencer's business, but overall she didn't know her potential customers, and despite receiving feedback that it was a great product, it wasn't *really* what they wanted.

DEFINING CUSTOMER PERSONAS

Now that research has been concluded, you should be able to define who your customers are. Customer personas are profiles of the different types of customers you have; these profiles will help you in making crucial business decisions — in the early days focus on one to two, as you can always add more personas as you go along. And don't worry about having more than one, it's normal because you will likely have customers with different needs but they all want your products.

When wanting to create profiles, consider the following things:

- Demographics
- Geographic

- Psychographic
- Behaviour

I segment according to psychographics; here are the kind of questions I try to find answers to in order to create customer profiles for the FWL brand:

- What do they care about?
- What are the problems they are experiencing?
- Who are the competitors and products/services they use?
- Who are the people that inspire them?
- Who influences their buying decisions?
- What music do they listen to?
- What are their aspirations?
- What social media platforms do they use often and what is their preferred means of consuming content?
- What is their lifestyle like?
- How do they like to learn?

These are just a few examples. Having this information allows you to effectively target your customer and create a product and marketing campaign that authentically connects with them. All this information can be gathered during the research phase via surveys, in interviews or through social media polls.

When I was setting out to develop a new product for FWL, I sent out a survey to find out more information about the existing community — I really do not want to create something that no one wants! I was very curious to understand what blogs my audience read, why they read them, how they prefer to learn — the direction of your questions really depends on your product or service. As a fashion brand with the mission 'making all women feel sexy' you may want to ask what music makes you feel sexy? Having insight into this could be a game-changer in your marketing.

I have three audience personas at FWL that I target, the first two being primary targets and the last being secondary:

- The Wannapreneur: A desire to become an entrepreneur but also striving for leadership positions in her 9–5.
- The Side Hustler: Works a 9–5 but also runs a business on the side and would potentially one day like to make her side hustle her main job.
- The Inspired One: Likes to listen to stories of women who have 'made it' and is always on the lookout for inspiring content.

I always refer back to these personas when making decisions around products, content or any important business decision — it gives focus.

GET TO WORK

1. What is your assumption?
2. What market research will you do and what information are you looking for?
3. What user research will you do and what are you looking out for?
4. Who are your competitors, what do they do and what don't they offer?
5. How can you create a better product?
6. What do your customers like about the competitors?
7. When can you start this research and how long will it take?
8. Once you have this research, can you move forward with your business idea?
9. Create one to two customer profiles based on your research.

JENNY GYLLANDER

Founder, Thingtesting

WHO IS JENNY GYLLANDER?

Jenny Gyllander is the Founder and CEO of Thingtesting, an independent brand discovery site where consumers can find and learn about new brands and get honest, unbiased recommendations among the deluge of D2C product launches. Committed to transparency, Founder and CEO Jenny Gyllander has grown the site from a brand-spotting Instagram account to a trustworthy go-to destination for online shoppers.

Prior to Thingtesting, Jenny worked at Backed VC, a London-based seed fund, and was the CMO of Slush, Europe's leading startup conference. Jenny is a Forbes 30 Under 30 alumni (2019), has been recognised as one of the top 100 Nordic leading figures in tech (The Nordic Web), and is a columnist for Courier Media.

JENNY'S STORY

The first year of Thingtesting, I spent zero time thinking about what it would become. I had no intention for it to be what it is today. I decided one night that I would learn to use Photoshop and post about the products I had thoughts on. At this time I had not identified that there was a big problem in the market, this was just a way for me to vent about products and showcase the new ones that I had come across – this was a purely organic idea with no strategy behind it, like how most side hustles tend to start out.

I never had plans to take Thingtesting on full time, but when you find something that you're passionate about, and you realise that it's become a solution to someone's problems, it becomes a dream to do so. The community grew quicker than I had expected and I started to get ideas on what to do for the next version of the Thingtesting platform from the community, they were making so many recommendations. When I went full time, in all honesty, it was not 100 per cent clear what the plan was. I didn't have the means to do entrepreneurship without any revenue in place. So what I did was create a 'close friends' membership, which was the tool that was convenient on Instagram to engage with a smaller group of people – this was an annual subscription. I shared with the community that they can support this cause by joining the subscription if they have enjoyed the content and want to continue to see it grow. I let them know that they'd be the first to know about what comes next.

I drew closer to the community by hosting meet-ups, dinners and events. I wanted to draw closer to the community – this was the reason behind creating the membership, plus it allowed me time to think about what the longer-term vision would be.

Over time, I had started to identify a bigger issue with the industry – there was no transparency in the consumer experience space. There needed to be honest reviews about products and easier ways to discover brands, as hundreds are launching daily. When you see a brand out there and you go to their website it's usually five-star reviews; the brand is in total control of what is being said. What I am building is a third-party destination where consumers and brands can engage in transparent dialogue. We are like Trustpilot for brands.

This led me to realise that the membership on Instagram was not enough to solve the problem I had identified. At that point, I decided to raise a $300,000 convertible note so I could focus on building something that would truly be a solution to the problem I had identified.

A big mission in the past year has been to remove my own personal brand from Thingtesting. This is mainly because the direct-to-consumer and online e-commerce space is so wide and the community wanted reviews from across several industries and categories – for example, pet products, men's and kids' products etc. – and this meant that I couldn't continue to do this alone. Me leading and being the voice of every review is not a scalable solution, so now I have freelance editors and creators who write for us. I am now focused on building the team and making sure we have the resources in place to support them and the business – it would be challenging for me to remain the face of the brand. I do not think it is sustainable. We are now a team of four, and we've been building Thingtesting.com for 10 months now, and have over 20k people using the site monthly.

In terms of our business model, we are not being paid by brands to review their products. Everything we showcase on Thingtesting is unbiased. Currently, we make the majority of our revenue from our newsletter partnerships. The plan is to continue to focus on the growth of the user base; that is a key priority for us and I'm pretty sure this will lead to more interesting revenue streams.

JENNY'S WORDS OF WISDOM

- If you're interested in something it's a good idea to say it out loud on the internet. There are many like-minded people that you'll discover through this. You'll never know where this will lead.
- The closer you stay to the community, the easier it becomes to identify the north star for your idea. Once you identify this, stay true to it and the values you create for your business.
- It should be fun; in the early beginnings do it for yourself before anyone else. If you're not passionate about your side hustle, I would rethink your idea.

@gyllanderjenny
@thingtesting
thingtesting.com

EXPERIMENTING: BUILDING AN MVP

'Done is better than perfect.'

There are several ways in which you can experiment with your idea. Most people use the tool and learning process called MVP (Minimum Viable Product). I titled this chapter experimenting to emphasise that this is not about building the final product but more about experimenting with your idea.

So what is it? MVPs were originally a concept coined by the tech industry, specifically for apps, but in my opinion this method can be used to test all types of ideas, products or services. In simple terms, MVPs are a way to create the most basic version of a product or service that can be released for consumers. An MVP might be a product, an app, a landing page or even a video — all of this can exist with no actual working product. It's a process of crafting the best solution to solve the problem, not an end product itself. As Eric Ries puts it: an MVP allows you to collect validated learning about customers with the least effort — the essence of an MVP is to find the right balance between what you are offering to users, and what the users actually need.

In the previous chapter, we looked at how to get research on your market and customer; you will use that information to build an MVP. The MVP provides you with information on how your customer feels about your product and service. The nature of the particular idea you have will determine how you go about testing it (see below for different types); if there isn't much uncertainty you may not need to bother with validating your assumption.

BUILD – MEASURE – LEARN

Build - measure - learn is the lean startup principle that continuously allows you to be at the forefront of change and evolvement; this is the process that we will be following here. The process is to build your MVP, measure the performance, then learn from it in order to build the final product. In some instances you may have to go through the cycle more than once to get the results you want. For example, with product samples, it's unlikely you will get it right the first time so you may need to do several rounds of testing.

A few MVP examples in action:

- Liv Little created gal-dem, a media company for women and people of colour that produces a bi-annual magazine and digital content. It first started out as a side hustle while she was at university, where she created a blog with friends sharing their experiences — she invested £20 in a theme and £100 to do their first magazine issue. Gal-dem is now a full-time media company with brand partnerships ranging from Nike to Sainsbury's to Bumble.
- Melanie Perkins created Canva, a free online graphic design platform. The idea started after she became frustrated with

how long it took to create a brochure and after giving students lessons on how to use design software. Her first business in response to the problem was Fusion Books, which allowed students to design their own yearbook — the business still exists today. Off the back of this idea, Canva was born, as she knew the tool could serve more than just those in the yearbook market. The lesson here is that sometimes your previous business could play a part in your MVP process.

- Lana Elie created Floom, an online marketplace dedicated to connecting customers from all over the UK who want unique and seasonal floral arrangements with local, independent florists who can provide both a bespoke work of art and same-day delivery. The idea first started as an Instagram page (the business did not have a name for the first six months). Lana would take a picture in her living room showcasing a flower, share details about the plant and what it represents. This was all the Instagram feed consisted of. She then used this content to push people to her landing page. The account quickly grew to 6,000 followers who then signed up to the email list. In her interview with *Entrepreneur*, Lana said, 'Use [Instagram] as a testing base before building too much of anything else. That's what helped me get my funding in the beginning, because then I had an Instagram account to prove user engagement and user need.'[14]

- Koreen Odiney created We're Not Really Strangers – an aesthetically pleasing viral Instagram account sharing inspirational quotes, feelings and thoughts — a few years on and it has now been gamified into a box of card games for

---

[14] www.entrepreneur.com/slideshow/298111

meaningful connections and conversations. It started with her sharing quotes around hers and others' deep feelings. The first game of WNRS was played with handwritten index cards in a park — as she says, 'Take small beginnings seriously.'[15]

- Dropbox started with a simple product video that explained what the founders wanted to launch. The video allowed them to connect with potential customers and overnight they attracted over 70,000 email sign-ups from people who wanted the product. This allowed them to get feed-back, which validated their assumptions and allowed them to create the final product.

- Zalando is an e-commerce platform that started with just an online storefront consisting of pictures of shoes from other shoe stores. When someone would buy a pair of shoes, an employee would then go and get those shoes from the actual store and ship them off to the customer — at this time there was no e-commerce or warehouse, just a landing page and one person in logistics.

- Airbnb, the most famous example on this list, is an online marketplace which enables people to rent out their properties or spare rooms to guests. With no money to start the business, the founders used their own apart-ment to validate their idea. They created a minimalist website, published photos and other details about their property, and found several paying guests almost

---

[15] www.forbes.com/sites/karineldor/2020/05/27/how-the-25-year-old-founder -of-were-not-really-strangers-created-a-global-movement-from-a-card-game -and-instagram-feed/?sh=61cb05123f99

immediately. This was just the beginning of something that was going to change how we experience travel and accommodation.

Remember that an MVP is an experiment — that means it can be conducted in as many creative ways as possible and more than once. Whatever you decide on, what you do must help in validating your assumption that your idea makes.

Even though your MVP might not be as lavish as you want it to be, this does not mean it should be mediocre. It still has your name and company's reputation attached to it. The goal of the MVP is simply to start small and work your way up from there.

EXISTING BUSINESSES

MVPs are not just for new business ideas, they can also be used for existing businesses that want to expand and introduce more products, features or services. Running an experiment in this case would be easier as you already have a user base to work with and a channel of communication.

BENEFITS OF HAVING AN MVP

- It's quicker to bring to life as it won't take as much time as building a complete product.
- It will help you see whether your idea is of interest to people.

- You can minimise the risk or likelihood of errors you could experience with your product.
- It helps you establish a user base of early adopters.
- An MVP provides an avenue to receive feedback from potential customers.
- When trying to gauge people's feelings, surveys will not do the best job as people find it hard to assess their feelings, whereas an MVP can help in looking at the action they took and did not take, which is more accurate than a survey in understanding behaviour.
- An MVP can produce revenue if people are willing to buy the product or service with a pre-order.

TYPES OF MVPS TO BUILD

When deciding on an MVP, be clear about what you want to achieve, what your goals are and what success looks like to you.

Landing page

In the form of a pitch, share a short description of what you are offering, including pricing if possible, then ask potential customers to sign up to find out more about updates. The amount of people that sign up can help you understand supply and demand, and you can also contact these people for feedback and start building a community before having an actual product. You can include share buttons on the landing page so that customers can share the landing page with their friends and family. You could also consider offering a discount code when someone signs up through a referral link. Think of fun creative incentives — you can offer all this while there is no product or service available but you are working on it in the background.

Trials/samples of physical prototype

This is where you create a sample of what to expect, which you can then decide to showcase on your social media platforms and you could allow users to sample or trial the product. For example, as a fashion brand you could make a sample of three items, take product shots and allow people to pre-order. These samples can also be sent to influencers to showcase your product and drive traffic to your site. During this time, you'll work on making the product perfect and address any concerns raised by testers.

Social media

As with Floom, a large social following in response to sharing your idea is a good sign that people are interested in it but it does not always mean they will buy it – the example I gave earlier about the influencer is a learning that we should all take on board. You can also use social media advertising to test ideas and see the response; for example, you can have two adverts that show the same product in different colours, and the one with the most clickthroughs and engagement can be the one you decide to produce.

Video explainer

A video is a great visual way to share your idea and explain what it is you are working on. This could cover its features, the founder's story and pricing. To add a touch of connection, it would be best to narrate the video yourself. The response can help with interest; after gathering feedback you can start to work on the idea. In Dropbox's case they were able to go to investors after the response they had received with their video; they also included jokes and humorous references within the video which did help in getting early adopters.[16]

Crowdfunding platform

Crowdfunding platforms like Kickstarter are used to help raise money for an idea. They allow you to upload information about your idea alongside visuals. The idea is validated as payments are received before the product is built, and in some cases you can pre-order the product and receive bonus items. This option allows you to build your product without spending a dime, you just need to make sure you can market the crowd-funding page well. The *Harvard Business Review* shared that Kickstarter campaigns that included videos are 85 per cent more likely to reach their funding goals than projects that do

---

[16] *The Lean Startup*, Eric Riles, p.99

not, because these videos help you leave an impression. They found that self-promotion (boasting or demonstrating skills and experience) and exemplification (appearing dedicated and hardworking) boosted success.[17]

A/B Test

A/B testing – otherwise known as split testing – is where you make different versions of adverts, campaigns or landing pages to see which one performs well and has the best response. This can help you test several ways of positioning or speaking about your product to get the best consumer result.

Content: events, podcasts and newsletters

If you can pull in a large number of people to discuss a topic around which you want to start a business, this could be a good sign that they would be interested in a product focused on this. For example, hosting panel events around women's health, specifically periods, could help you learn what women are experiencing and also allow you to showcase the idea you have in mind to solve their problems. This could be an event, a podcast or even a weekly newsletter before you release the product or service.

Pop-up shop

These are shops that are open for a certain period of time; it is an opportunity to see how many people will interact with your

---

[17] 'How To Change Anyone's Mind', *Harvard Business Review*, Volume 99, Issue 2

product or service. You can have a pop-up stand at an event that is relevant to your customers or hire a short-let store to showcase and sell your products or services.

The concierge MVP[18]

Use humans before automation comes in. For a service-based business with the aims of scaling, in the beginning you can decide to focus on a very small number of orders and do things manually. For example, OjaHQ, a food delivery service founded by Mariam Jimoh, seeks to make ethnic foods readily available by connecting local multicultural stores with customers. In its very early days for the MVP, Mariam partnered with one store only and delivered within a 10-mile radius. Mariam picked up the products from the store and delivered them directly to the customers' doors. She obviously cannot scale this process but it gave her the opportunity to work on a solution, such as logistics, and provided her with valuable insight from her customers as she met with them one on one.

The Wizard of Oz MVP

Where an idea is based around technology, such as AI, you can do things manually in the test phase with a human performing what the machine would usually do automatically. Tiffany Dufu created The Cru, a peer-coaching platform for women looking to accelerate their professional and personal growth. The platform uses AI to connect eight women together to form a 'Cru' — these

---

[18] *The Lean Startup*, Eric Riles, p.99

women come from diverse industries and are matched based on values, personality and demographics to form a Cru that holds regular, structured gatherings. You and your Cru members act as a mutual support system as each of you moves towards your goals. She initially had a landing page which featured a video about what to expect from the service and a SurveyMonkey questionnaire to gather from women the info she needed — she hit 500 women in signups and asked someone in her network to help her interview the women one on one over the summer. It was a tough experience but she felt the need to validate her hypothesis with these interviews and match 100 of these women manually. Tiffany and two women in her network printed out all 100 profiles, laid them out on the floor and matched women; they had recorded this process, and it later became the infrastructure for her algorithm. Tiffany then went on to raise some funding and was able to scale the platform so that she could use AI to automatically match women and scale the platform. This is a great example of how non-tech people can validate a tech product.

GETTING THE WORD OUT ABOUT YOUR MVP

I cover promoting your product in more detail in the Getting Your Side Hustle Known chapter. Here are some brief tips for your MVP:

- Share your idea with relevant blogs and news sites.

- Share with communities that have a similar audience – this could be organic or paid and could be via newsletters, podcasts, articles, Facebook groups, Slack channels, etc.
- Reveal your product to your network with an incentive of using a referral link to gain gifts, discounts, etc., for pre-orders.

MEASURING THE SUCCESS OF YOUR MVP

Once you launch your MVP, listen to what your customers tell you in their feedback and develop another MVP if you need to. All of this information will help you develop the product that your customers want.

When measuring the success of your MVP, it will differ depending on the type of MVP you created. In order to measure its success you will need to define the metrics that matter to your idea.

Analytics

Tools like Crazy Egg and Google Analytics allow you to view the interaction on your landing page; this could be heatmaps that allow you to understand where people are scrolling to on the page, where they drop off, where people are clicking the most, etc. This information can allow you to develop a better landing page and understand customers' behaviour better.

Communication

Conduct customer interviews and find out what your customers felt about the experiment, if they think your product will help them solve their problem, and where it can be improved. Be creative in how you communicate with your customers: this can range from interviews to email conversations down to social media polls, but overall the best option would be anything face-to-face.

Signups/waiting list

The number of people that sign up to the waiting list is a good indicator that people are interested in your product.

Number of click-throughs and conversions

This is the number of people that click a link and convert to a customer. This could be a link that you share in a social media advert where a customer signs up for a trial or demo product.

Number of downloads

The number of people that have downloaded your app at the beginning of the journey. This number is important and will continue to be important, but in order for it not to be a vanity metric there needs to be growth in the quantity of downloads and engagement with the app.

User engagement

Although the MVP is being downloaded, how many of the users are active? Above everything, engagement is what you should be driving and looking out for. Once you have good engagement, ask yourself how you can increase the users and the engagement. These early adopters are the ones that will help your business idea succeed, so you should consider this and think about how you can turn passive users into engaged ones.

Observation

Observing how your customers interact with or react to the MVP is a great way to measure success. For example, if you have a clothing brand, when you have some samples, observe how your customers wear the clothes. Are they struggling to get them on? Do they look and feel comfortable? Does it look as you desired? Levi's have been known to create the best type of jeans; regardless of the size they come in, they are always comfortable. It's apparent that the company have invested time in understanding their customers' bodies and creating a product that fits well.

Number of paying users

How many people have parted with their money is an excellent marker of success, whether this is through pre-orders or donating to your crowdfunding campaign. This action shows a high level of interest in and commitment to your idea.

IMPORTANT NOTES ON MEASURING YOUR MVP

Some metrics are more important than others at different stages of your idea. This will require you to change the expectations you have for each metric and define success at each stage.

Vanity metrics

These are the things that you should not be marking as signs of success. Vanity metrics are things you can measure that don't matter; you simply can't make decisions based on these, as they're easily changed or manipulated, and they don't bear a direct correlation with numbers that speak to business success.[19]

Personally, I feel at some stages this may look like success but as the product journey progresses the signs for success change. One could be website hits in the early days but as time goes on you need to start focusing on how many of those hits are actually converting to customers.

A new community app had announced that they had hit 10,000 app downloads. I was so impressed but when I went into the app I only saw one to three comments or no comments at all on community posts. The essence of the app is to drive conversation and build community with these posts, so it's important that there is engagement. The download numbers were high, but the engagement was low, so is this a metric that

---

[19] https://www.crazyegg.com/blog/glossary/what-is-a-vanity-metric

should be used as a sign of success? What should be measured here is engagement metrics and not downloads, as they are vanity metrics, but in the early days they can serve well. You'll need to look into why your downloads are high and engagement is low; something could be wrong.

LEARN

Now that you have all the information from the market and user research and from the MVP test, you need to conclude what the next steps will be. Will you continue to go through the three-step model – build, measure, learn – in order to get closer to the best solution to solve the problem? If you feel you have created the best solution then crack on with developing the full product but make sure you are still open to feedback. If you feel you haven't then you may need to repeat this process or even pivot your idea.

STAY OBSESSED WITH YOUR CUSTOMER

As long as you hope to be successful with your idea then you will need to be continuously talking to your customer even after you have a product that has been launched. Market and customer research and analysis should be something that you are committed to doing long term – it should never end – as this is how businesses stay relevant. You must keep engaging with your customers and garnering their feedback in order to stay relevant, especially as new technology is being created and changing how we do everything every year. So you must continue to check how you are speaking to customers, how you are selling, where you are selling as all these details count towards improving your brand. Interact with your customers in creative ways via social media polls, yearly surveys, community groups or email — this allows you to do research in a quick and easy way.

YOU ARE 30 PER CENT MORE LIKELY TO SUCCEED

The good news for side hustlers like you living in 2021 and beyond is that your small business is 30 per cent more likely to survive — the small-business failure rate since 1977 has declined by 30 per cent. According to Scott Shane, professor of Entrepreneurial Studies at Case Western Reserve University, this is due to would-be entrepreneurs evaluating their ideas more carefully before taking the plunge.[20] Which leads me to my next point . . .

THE MOST COMMON REASON WHY YOU COULD FAIL

There are so many reasons why a small business could fail, but the most common (at number one out of 20), according to

---

[20] www.entrepreneur.com/article/254871

CB Insights, is simply that the market does not need the product. No amount of marketing or investment can help a product that is not needed. Research shows that 21.5 per cent of small businesses fail after just a year. About half of all small businesses make it to their fifth year of work, while only a third survive a decade.[21]

THINGS TO NOTE

Do not get caught up with the MVP step. This is where the majority of people slow down because they are *trying* to build the perfect experiment; the quicker you can get something out into the world and hear from customers, the better. For the procrastinators, you may decide to hide behind 'I'm a perfectionist' – no, you could be procrastinating and may be hiding behind the fear of not knowing if this will work or the feeling that you are not ready. As suggested previously, I would encourage you to have an accountability partner to make sure you are hitting the goals you need to. You have more chance of success if you launch than someone who decides to procrastinate and keep on testing.

This side-hustle journey is one that you cannot predict and that is the beauty of viewing it as an experiment. If your idea is solving a problem, then get that MVP out there and let customers tell you the same.

---

[21] www.cbinsights.com/research/startup-failure-reasons-top/

STEPS FOR AN MVP

- Write a hypothesis.
- Define the goals of your MVP.
- Build an MVP.
- Share the MVP.
- Measure your MVP for success.
- Analyse the data.
- Learn: repeat former steps, pivot or go big.

GET TO WORK

1. What is your hypothesis?
2. Has your hypothesis been validated? List the companies that are already doing this.
3. What MVP can you build in order to help you validate your idea? Create a timeline for how long it will take from build to test.
4. Try to discover how much time, money and effort it would take to create your MVP, through asking those who have created something similar and where you can't do this then I would suggest estimating.
5. How can you let people know about your MVP? What communities can you share this with? Make a list of ideas.

TANIA BOLER

Founder of Elvie

WHO IS TANIA BOLER?

Tania Boler is an internationally recognised women's health expert who is passionate about improving physical and emotional wellbeing while leading candid conversations around women's issues. As the CEO of Elvie, her mission has been to create world-class technology products that address women's intimate issues throughout every life stage. Tania has degrees from both Oxford and Stanford Universities; she completed a PhD in Sexual Reproductive Health and has published extensive research and several books on the subject.

Before partnering with Alexander Asseily to found Elvie in 2013, Tania was the Global Director of Research and Innovation at Marie Stopes International, focusing on sexual health in developing countries. Additionally, Tania worked extensively in Africa promoting research into maternal and reproductive health – with a specific focus on HIV and teenage pregnancy – and worked with the UN to launch the first-ever curriculum on Sexuality Education.

TANIA'S STORY

As a sexual health researcher who had previously worked for the UN and global NGOs, I've always been passionate about driving change in society, especially around neglected and taboo issues facing women during motherhood. While working at the UN, I began to recognise technology's potential to disrupt the way we think about health – and even quicken the pace at which change can occur.

The idea for Elvie Trainer, our first product, came to me when I was pregnant. While experiencing many changes in my body, I was shocked to discover that despite having worked in women's health for 15 years – across various fields and disciplines – there was so much I didn't know, especially when it came to my pelvic floor.

My husband is French, and when we were together in France I learned that it is common for French women to attend pelvic floor rehabilitation classes after birth to help re-strengthen their bodies. I couldn't believe that nothing like this existed in other countries, especially since I later found that one in three women will experience pelvic floor problems during their lifetime. And another huge problem? No one was talking about this issue. I was used to working on highly taboo topics and stigmatised issues – like HIV prevention and access to safe abortion – and pelvic floor weakness was another apparent topic that's 'hush-hush' in society.

As I began to research further, I quickly learned the shocking statistics relating to incontinence and prolapse, impacting half of all women over 50. I started conversations with researchers and physiotherapists to see what we could do to change this. Eventually, I realised that technological innovation was lacking in this area, and most of what was on the market at the time for women was simply ineffective. Giving women real-time biofeedback is the most reliable way to encourage commitment to pelvic floor training, yet this technology was only available in hospitals. It became evident that not only did we need to create a product that addressed this, but we needed to challenge the cultural norms that have forbidden women to talk openly about their bodies.

I had never planned to start a business or get involved in tech. However, with this apparent gap in women's health, I set out to create a smart Kegel trainer and app that could give users the same real-time biofeedback that seemed so inaccessible – all while making it fun, convenient and effective. I knew that we were onto something and had the potential to empower women to take control of their health and wellbeing. So, in the fall of 2015, we launched Elvie Trainer.

Launching a Kegel trainer wasn't cut and dry – and it certainly was not easy! When I began, there wasn't even the term 'femtech'. So, when pitching to investors (a majority of whom were men), it was hard work to sell them on the notion that women will talk openly about pelvic floor health. At one point, I was even told that women's health products were 'too niche', which was certainly hard to fathom – especially with the potential that these tools have of addressing the needs of 51 per cent of the global population. It took me a few fundraising meetings to realise that I needed to be upfront about women's issues and not skirt around words like 'vagina' or other topics with the potential to make investors uncomfortable. Now, when meeting with prospective investors, I like to see their reaction once I say the 'V' word. I call this the 'vagina test'! It's a fun and easy way to gauge whether we'll be a good fit for one another.

Beyond attracting investors, our most significant obstacles came with building our technology. For example, designing one solution that could truly solve breastfeeding problems that women have been enduring for far too long! My business partner, Alexander, encouraged hiring top engineers from the word 'go'. As you scale, this is extremely important. You need to surround yourself with people who believe in the mission as much as you do and are the best at doing the jobs you need to do. So we set out to hire world-class female designers who understood women's needs, placed them at the heart of the design process, and created beautiful products that offered women the best solution out there.

Carving out space in a male-centric world is never easy, and it can be intimidating to jump into something when you haven't seen many examples set by other female friends or leaders. However, there is a growing network of extraordinary, like-minded female entrepreneurs out there who are willing to support you and help you to make essential connections.

I would also say as well as living and breathing your mission, you (sometimes) need to have skin like a rhino alongside. It's all about not taking anything too personally. It can be hard to hear criticism about something you're so passionate about and have worked so hard for, but sometimes this is what you need to hear for positive change.

Financially, one of the most empowering moments was when we successfully closed on the most significant funding round in femtech history, securing $42 million in Series B funding in April 2019. This investment gave the company confidence in our mission while paving the way for us to expand our global business and team to nearly 150 employees. We've also been able to bring out new game-changing products like Elvie Curve and Elvie Catch to market.

My other proudest achievements to date have been the conversations we have started that empower women to talk about their health, breaking decades-old taboos in the process. Whether it is helping women talk about their struggles with bladder weakness or giving mothers the flexibility they need to get on with their lives, Elvie's work isn't just in technology; it is a woman's empowerment movement that gets people talking openly. Watching this shift in mentality surrounding women's health and wellness – with Elvie being a vital part of this change – has been fascinating. Ultimately, women don't just deserve better tech, they're demanding it, and with all the untapped potential in this industry, we want to keep building on this early success and continue to pioneer products that shatter our assumptions of what's possible. Going forward, there are still very severe gender gaps in mainstream medicine, and it's essential (and exciting) to explore opportunities to create a paradigm shift in this space.

TANIA'S WORDS OF WISDOM

- One important thing I've learned is to embrace rejection. Developing the best products and inspiring support from the right investors takes time, dedication and plenty of rejection! But if you believe in the mission, you can take these moments of doubt to reflect and rethink how you can build a better way forward.
- Another piece of advice would be 'feel the fear and push through it'. Because the best things in life often happen when you step out of your comfort zone. There have been countless times when I've second-guessed myself or even felt sick to my stomach with fear, but I carried on. Elvie wouldn't have started if I hadn't embraced my nerves. Now, we're breaking barriers and letting women know that there's nothing that should hold them back.
- Finally, I remind myself constantly that my mission comes first and try not to take anything too personally. The more open I can be to criticism, the more room I have for an objective perspective, and I can appreciate constructive feedback that takes my ideas further.

@tania.boler
@elvie
elvie.com

IT TAKES A VILLAGE

'Know your limits and know when to get help.'

We've all read those articles that talk about how someone got started, how they 'made it happen', but the people they rarely ever talk about are the ones that actually made the business run — whether it be freelancers, consultants or part-time/full-time staff. And truth be told this was your idea and your story to tell, so we don't necessarily need to hear about them but what we do need to do is paint a realistic picture of how a business is run and the resources it takes to maintain it before you can even think of scaling it.

Bringing other people in to help run your side hustle requires time and patience, but if you've worked a job before then you know that it takes time for a team to gel and find the best ways of working together. You might be thinking, 'Why would I spend my time managing people?', well, so you can create more time to do other things — and apart from people who you could hire, in this chapter I'll also discuss co-founders.

This chapter is most important if you plan on maintaining your full-time job while running your side hustle. This is the key to keeping the business afloat, aside from finding ways to automate your business.

CO-FOUNDERS

I've co-founded two businesses in the past and if I knew then what I know now I would have done several things differently. There are so many reasons why it's great to have a co-founder, but some ideas really don't need one; they may require you to get a freelancer or hire a consultant instead. It sounds fun wanting to start a business with your friend or maybe even your partner, as you get to spend time with someone you like and get on with, but there are several difficult dynamics to take into consideration. Having a co-founder is like being in a marriage, it really is not the same as having a colleague at work.

WHY YOU SHOULD BE CONSIDERING A CO-FOUNDER

There are a few good reasons why you should consider getting on board a co-founder, but there are also a few key things to have in place if you do decide to go down this route.

They have the missing skill: They simply have what it takes for the business to get going, the skill that you don't have. We all have strengths and different backgrounds, we just can't have everything, and in some instances that one thing you don't have is a fundamental part of getting your idea off the ground. For example, if your idea is heavily dependent on technology, say, an app is probably needed, then the likelihood is you'll have to outsource this, which can be pretty expensive, or you could decide to bring on a technical co-founder who will bear the risk with you and create the app. When deciding on bringing in a co-founder for this purpose, you have to weigh up how important this skill is to your business.

Divide responsibilities: Two people will always be quicker than one, and bringing on someone who is as keen and eager as you will help in seeing progress at a faster rate. You should split responsibilities according to your strengths and expertise.

Splitting the risk: Without a doubt, starting a business could be high risk, it may require a large input of money, and having someone to share that risk with you will lighten the burden and the blow if all things don't go right.

Although you could hire people to do the above things, hires will never have the same passion, grit and dedication that a co-founder would have and neither can you give them as much control and responsibility as you could a co-founder. Well, not in the early days!

THINGS TO HAVE IN PLACE FOR A CO-FOUNDER

Make sure you are aligned on vision and values: This should not be an afterthought, it's an important requirement in order for you both to see eye to eye and for the business to thrive and go in one direction – this will definitely make things smoother and make decision-making easier. For instance, if you are starting an ethical fashion brand and one of you is more concerned about making quick money (even if it requires being unethical) and the other is committed to staying ethical and doing things right, these opposing views will hold the business back from being a success.

Have contracts in place: It sounds like a no-brainer, but the amount of people who have started something that was once an idea and is now a fully fledged business who don't have contracts? They are many – and I was one! This may not need to be discussed in the early stages but the earlier the better and, if possible, ask a lawyer to help you look over it. This contract should cover all the 'what ifs?', responsibilities, titles and shares, leaving nothing for you both to be guessing about.

Have respect and trust: Without trust, there is no success — this is crucial to the success of your partnership and your business. Trust is like glass: once smashed it is very hard to put back together – in fact, more or less impossible. Trust can be built over time, so don't fret too much if you are just meeting the person; I'd say take your time and let the trust develop.

Leave no room for confusion: Be clear from day one on everything necessary, such as how you like to work, the best forms of communication for you and boundaries you have for work.

A clear outline of roles, responsibilities AND expectations: From my experience when these three things are not clearly outlined it can cause a lot of friction; no one wants anyone stepping on their feet or micromanaging them. As co-founders you are partners and you both have your strengths and weaknesses, so make sure you align yourself with the role(s) that fit you best and in some instances you may be both doing the same thing in order to 'divide and conquer'.

Other important things like shares and titles can be covered in your contract; again, I would suggest you seek legal counsel and speak to experienced founders to see how they have approached this process.

WORKING WITH FRIENDS

This is an unspoken topic and one I will touch on very briefly. Treat them like you would any business partner – which means, yes, share the contracts but above all believe in their professional ability to deliver on their commitments. There's no point in partnering up just because you are friends; that's a recipe for failure if you ask me.

An advantage of being friends is that you won't be starting from scratch; you know one another well, know how you each handle stress, how you prefer to work, etc., or maybe you don't but nonetheless there's still some familiarity. You won't always agree on things, and that is completely fine. You don't want a yes person, you need someone who will challenge you.

BUILDING A TEAM

A big piece of advice here is to try to keep your team as lean as possible; we tend to think that the size of our team determines how 'successful' the business is, but it really doesn't. Only bring in the most necessary people to help with the things you can't do because of lack of skill or time. And before you think of hiring someone to do something for you, ask yourself: 'Can I automate this?', meaning, can you find a way to have this task done automatically through technology? I mention this under the productivity section.

Document the process: At different points of running FWL, I have brought people on board to manage content, plan events and respond to emails. Where possible, I have tried to document the process because this allows the individual to have strict guidelines on what to do and what not to do. For example, with our newsletter, I have a document that lays out what the content focus is, how to send out the newsletter (step by step) and how to analyse the newsletter after. This saves me time in taking someone through it, because I can instead ask them to look through the guide, digest and present their questions to me if they have any. The process should be written in chronological order and can also be accompanied by explanations such as 'why' this must be done and 'what' will happen if not. Towards the end you may decide to leave FAQs, which could cover all the usual questions that get asked. Tools like Loom are brilliant if you need to create a video recording of the process.

Get the law off your back: In the early days you really don't want to be bringing in employees as this requires you to have to deal with so many different employment rights. You should be looking at freelancers as they are responsible for themselves; it sounds a little harsh, but you really don't need this responsibility in a side hustle.

Internships/work experience: These are people looking for hands-on work experience. If you can offer this to them without having to heavily micromanage them and as a way of supporting upcoming talent, this is a great option. Due to not being as experienced, they are typically much more affordable to hire –

yes, you should pay interns and those doing work experience with you! There are a few organisations that can match you with interns, such as Lunatalents.com, run by founder Lu Li, or findyourintern.com, run by founder Jasmine MacPhee.

Protect your IP and business: When sharing information with the people you hire or outsource to, protect yourself by asking them to sign NDAs and create agreements that cover the work they do for you. For example, when I used to hire contributing writers for our blog, all the content they produced was owned by FWL – this was included in an agreement I had with all the writers.

Decide on the best ways of working: From the get-go, try to understand the best methods of working together and how you'd like to communicate. It may be that you meet every Thursday evening to discuss high-priority tasks or that you communicate strictly via email or Slack.

Understand boundaries: It's important that you know the boundaries with each person you hire: What are their cut-off times for contacting them? Are they comfortable with you contacting them via social media or WhatsApp?

HOW TO HIRE A TEAM

Whether you're looking for a co-founder or people to hire to support your side hustle, here are a few ways to go about finding the right person.

Ask mentors/advisors: It's likely they could be mentoring someone who would be the perfect match for you. There was an instance when a mentor of mine connected me with a potential co-founder when she realised we both had the same missions.

Use skill-specific job boards: For example, if you are looking for a marketer then you could consider using job boards focused on marketers. This allows you to reach a pool of candidates that have the skill set for which you are hiring.

Network in and outside of your circle: Get the word out through family, friends and your network.

Join skill-specific communities: If you are seeking a developer, join communities focused on tech or developers.

Use social media: Put the word out, whether it be through a status update on LinkedIn or a tweet on Twitter, push the word far and wide. The internet does wonders in spreading messages.

I know it may seem like this takes all the fun out of starting a side hustle but it saves you from having less fun later on — I've seen many have to shut down or teams part ways because some of these important things were not put in place in the beginning.

HIRE FAST, FIRE FAST

You're not going to hire the right people on the first go, especially if you're not very clear on what you are looking for. This process tends to be hit and miss and requires experience to get it right.

When you've realised you have hired the wrong person, don't waste your time analysing the situation; make the quick decision to let them go. A bad hire can do a lot of damage to your small business and you also don't have the money to waste – you are not a big corporation with that luxury.

GET TO WORK

1. What are the major skills needed for your business that a co-founder could bring?
2. Who do you know that matches the skills you have listed to the above question?
3. What are the day-to-day tasks you need support with?
4. How much money are you willing to put towards hiring people on a monthly basis and how many hours would it require for them to do the tasks?

ABADESI OSUNSADE

Founder & CEO of Hustle Crew and VP @ BrandWatch

WHO IS ABADESI?

Abadesi Osunsade is the founder of Hustle Crew, a career-advancement community for the underrepresented in tech and author of careers advice book Dream Big. Hustle Hard: The Millennial Woman's Guide to Success in Tech. *She campaigns tirelessly for a more inclusive tech sector to ensure the injustices of the present aren't cemented into the future through the product's tech creates. Abadesi was a team leader in growth-oriented roles at Amazon, HotelTonight and Groupon, where she joined as one of the first partner managers and helped scale the department five times in her first eight months. She currently works at Brandwatch as VP of Community & Belonging.*

ABADESI'S STORY

I quit my job at a startup with no next moves planned — I was tired of what I was experiencing as a Black woman in tech and literally being the only one in my team. I realised there was an urgent need to address the fact that tech teams do not reflect the society they serve and this means the lack of representation will *lead to bias. This lack of representation goes untalked about and unaddressed. There needed to be a conversation around how individuals in the tech world can be more aware of their bias, as well as systemic bias, so they can create more equitable organisations and make better equitable decisions in their lives — in comes Hustle Crew, a careers community and a training company.*

The first version of Hustle Crew had workshops for women in tech. *I also used this opportunity to make sure we all built connections and networked together. A lot of the community members make introductions to their organisations, which is a big gain for us and helps reduce the need to cold sell.*

After a while, we decided that this was no longer about women *but anyone who wants to support the mission, and men decided to get involved. From those workshops, Hustle Crew turned into a newsletter where we share career updates, jobs, news — the community just grew and grew.*

When Hustle Crew first started, it was very much community focused *— supporting people with their careers. Although we used a subscription model to offer coaching services to community members, it was much harder to maintain a steady income as a B2C business. Now we have decided to approach organisations because they also need to address the bias in their companies — that's why they haven't been able to increase diversity or retain them. We sell culture change support. In those six months as a B2C company I learned that I needed to change the model to B2B, it was also a better revenue stream as it's harder to reach new customers with a consumer-focused company that is* bootstrapped. Marketing is expensive. With B2B where I worked with the organisations, I was then able to recruit their employees to join our community – this model just worked so much better.

The real turning point for my company was 2020, following the tragic deaths of George Floyd and Breonna Taylor. That moment caused organisations to wake up and address their issues around bias and consider the importance of educating themselves on anti-bias strategies, anti-racism policies and topics that would make the workplace more inclusive for everyone. This is when we finally saw demand for the training products increase. We also brought back in the B2C model and launched a premium subscription which allowed change agents within their communities to access monthly resources to help support their work and build them up. This has become an additional revenue stream for the company, which is now turning over six figures.

I'm now in a full-time role as a VP in a tech company doing the work that I do with my side hustle. At every stage of Hustle Crew, where there has been an opportunity to hire freelancers or consultants, I have to continue to do this – the fact that I run a careers community means I have access to great talent. I put a call out for extra hands, looked at the talent in the community and hired people accordingly. A lot of the operational stuff I am still doing I decided to offload to one of the freelancers so I could maintain my job. I also hire consultants to run the workshops as I am less available. The team have been happy to focus and build up Hustle Crew; I now only focus on supporting the business with sales where clients *need more convincing. I'm extremely grateful for the incredible women behind the scenes who keep Hustle Crew running.*

It's important to acknowledge that I'm in a privileged position where I don't have to take a salary from Hustle Crew. *I started the company as a full-time founder; it was extremely hard financially for me to live on it, which is why it became a side hustle. I was a full-time founder for one year and it's now been my side hustle for three years — I've made a choice that I want to keep it this way and I can do that by hiring incredible women and investing in them and their futures – this is part of the mission, so it's perfect. There are several senior leaders in organisations with side hustles or roles. You can get to a point in your career where your expertise is so valued and you are able to offer this on the side of your full-time role.*

ABADESI'S WORDS OF WISDOM

- Focus on your obsession.
- Set realistic expectations, such as how long will it take to build an audience, make your first sale, be profitable, etc.
- Define what success looks like and be willing to adapt that!

@abadesi
@hustlecrewlive
hustlecrew.co

3

BRANDING YOUR IDEA

This part looks at how business ideas become brands, something you need to be thinking about before you launch or engage your customers, argues Emily Heyward, founder of Red Antler. Her advice goes against the idea of the lean startup process we discussed in the ideas section, but I also believe they can both be worked on simultaneously; you can be building a brand whilst testing out the idea.

So, what is a brand? It's more than a logo, that's for sure; it's a combination of the look and feel of a business — you know the emotions you get when you think of a business, see their adverts or see their products? All of that combined is brand. But more deeply a brand is the perception that people have of your company through all these elements. In order to control that perception, we need to weave the details such as the why, the values and how you speak to the customer into the business.

Brand never used to be an essential aspect when bringing a business idea to life, but now when we look around we know that it plays a strong role in making you not only stand out in a sea of the new businesses opening every minute (just scroll through Instagram and you'll see your friend launching something new or a sponsored ad from a brand you've never heard of) but it also plays a huge part in turning potential customers into raving fans, sometimes before you even officially have a product to sell.

As we go into the next couple of chapters, start to think about what you want your side hustle to stand for, how you want it to look and how you want people to feel when they engage with it.

IT'S MORE THAN MAKING A SALE

*'Nowadays people are looking for brands that make
a difference, not just brands that have
great products.'*

When you close your eyes and think of the brands that you truly admire – the ones that make you feel something, that speak to your core beliefs – they are likely to be ones that have a strong purpose at the heart of what they do. These brands not only offer great products but they inspire us – they inspire us to want to believe in something bigger, like purpose, and to want to stand for something. While profit is generally the driving force for setting up your startup, success for these types of brands meets at the intersection of profit and purpose.

You might be wondering, what does this have to do with your side hustle? You're just a one-woman team, so why does something like purpose matter to such a small business? Purpose is the first thing you need to establish when building a brand, as this is what gives small businesses strength and an edge. It's what empowered Dollar Shave Club, a subscription business founded in 2011 to threaten Gillette, a brand that is close to 100 years old.

WHAT IS A PURPOSE-DRIVEN BRAND?

A purpose-driven brand is a business that stands for something bigger than a product or a service, something that goes beyond profit. This is their core motivation to deliver to their customers, it is why they have started the journey of the organisation and it gives them their competitive edge in a saturated market.

MYTHS ABOUT PURPOSE-DRIVEN BRANDS

- Purpose is only for charities or when doing Corporate Social Responsibility (CSR) projects: A charity is created for a social purpose and a brand purpose in this instance does not have to be social, it is a mission on which an organisation is focused, and even if it is social, it does not make your organisation a charity. A typical example is Apple, with 'doing things differently', then there's Nike, with 'unite the world through sport to create a healthy planet, active communities and an equal playing field for all'.
- It's just a marketing gimmick: This may be true for some organisations, and to me this is unethical, but the foundation of having a purpose as a business is not for marketing purposes, it's to help guide you towards a goal and give you a point of focus.
- Purpose will take away from selling and affect profit: Research has shown that brands that have a purpose are more likely to have brand loyalty from customers, which should result in great commercial success.

HAVING A PURPOSE

When thinking of the purpose of your brand, think of something that you're committed to driving towards — a statement that looks beyond the sale but wants to truly make a difference in the world. I believe that the purpose can't just be one for the brand but something that the founder truly believes in. Take for example, Beauty Stack, which I mentioned earlier; their mission is 'to provide economic empowerment for women', and currently they are doing this by building an online marketplace for independent beauty professionals through which they can sell their services to users. The business was created by a founder whose history demonstrates that she's passionate about economically empowering women — you can always tell when a mission really means something to the founder and is authentic. They've also hosted Beauty Stack business events to further equip their beauty professionals with business knowledge that would allow them to effectively run their businesses and scale.

WHY PURPOSE-DRIVEN BRANDS ARE SO IMPORTANT

- They help to communicate what the brand stands for: Customers appreciate it when brands are clear on what their stance is; they find that those who communicate their purpose are more attractive.[22]

---

[22] https://www.accenture.com/us-en/insights/strategy/brand-purpose?c=strat_competitiveagilnovalue_10437227&n=mrl_1118

- It is a competitive advantage: Whatever makes your business different from the competitor next door is partly down to your purpose. If it's one that aligns with your customers' values then you've hit gold.
- They turn customers into engaged fans: When a customer feels a personal connection, they will engage more in the content you create, buy your products and become advocates of your brand – free word-of-mouth marketing!
- This identity improves sales: As mentioned before, it improves the bottom line. This is not the objective of purpose but it is the impact it has on sales. Who wouldn't want to support a business that is doing good in the world? We are emotional beings and tend to put our money where we know it will serve a higher purpose. Research by Accenture has said that over 63 per cent of consumers prefer to shop with purpose-driven brands and 51 per cent expect you to stand for a cause,[23] and 80 per cent say they feel they are doing some good in the world when they buy from purpose-driven brands. These individuals are also likely to buy another product from you and switch over from a brand that has no purpose.
- Gives the founder drive when things get tough: Things will get tough but the purpose of why you started the company drives you to not want to give up and helps you to persevere.

---

[23] https://www.accenture.com/us-en/insights/strategy/brand-purpose?c=strat_competitiveagilnovalue_10437227&n=mrl_1118

- Not only builds customer loyalty but also internal loyalty from the team and attracts great talent: The purpose not only affects how customers feel but those you choose to work with – whether that is freelancers or temp hires, it gives them a sense of meaningfulness for the work that they do. At FWL, there have been several occasions where I have received emails in regards to women wanting to work with me or intern, and this has been down to the purpose and mission we have. That is what has attracted them.

WHY BRANDS WITH A PURPOSE LAST

Knowing early on that you want to be a purpose-led brand will determine how you do business, how you market to your customers, how you speak with them and maybe even how you choose your business model. The reason why small businesses or early-stage companies can outdo the big players is because they have won over customers through purpose — especially at a time when we as humans are questioning where we put our money. Being 'sustainable' should be more than a buzzword you use in your marketing but a guide to how your whole supply chain operates.

When founder Shope Delano shared a post with her followers on Instagram about her new workwear brand, *Kind Regards* – 'clothes and conversations for self-defined working women' – it immediately struck a chord with her followers. Her post was in the style of an open letter and espoused her brand's mission and values while calling out the many ways in which work is unfair to women. The post went viral. There was no product on offer yet, but the women she was targeting felt heard and seen. Shope's background is in brand marketing; she combined this knowledge with her own following of 20k to create social buzz. When I spoke with Shope she emphasised that she is being intentional about organically building her brand audience-first.

More and more big organisations are trying to tie purpose into their marketing as they know this is what wins people over and they feel threatened by this when they see small businesses taking share of the market. In my opinion it's why the big fast-moving consumer goods such as Unilever and Procter & Gamble have bought over so many small businesses. But the advantage you have as a side-hustler, one-woman team is speaking directly to your customers and letting them hear your voice, because you as the founder are the driver of that purpose.

The purpose statement is at the centre of all your decisions and a guiding force as to how you do business.

YOU MUST STAND FOR SOMETHING

Nowadays we are all starting to hold big brands accountable for how they run their business, and the same is expected from all businesses, whether big or small, and this is something you should keep in mind when starting a brand — you must uphold what you said you stand for and are committed to.

Although your purpose may not be tied to a social purpose, there is now an expectation for brands to stand for some societal issues. Research has shown that when businesses stand for nothing, 48 per cent of consumers will criticise them and 42 per cent will walk away[24] – that is a huge number of customers. 'What does this brand stand for?' is now a part of the decision process when a consumer wants to make a purchase; they are even willing to switch brands if they feel a personal connection with one.

HOW TO CREATE A PURPOSE-DRIVEN BUSINESS

- Think about why you really started and make this your core purpose.
- Define the change you want to make in the customers' life, industry or the world.
- Incorporate the why and the purpose into your messaging by creating key messages, then use this within all your communications, such as email and social media captions.
- Be genuine and authentic – we can all tell when a brand is not who they say they are.

---

[24] https://www.accenture.com/us-en/insights/strategy/brand-purpose?c=strat_competitiveagilnovalue_10437227&n=mrl_1118

- Be human – make sure to humanise your brand with relatable content.
- Articulate the why with your audience consistently.
- Ask for feedback.

GET TO WORK

1. List three brands with which you feel a personal connection.
2. What is it that makes you feel connected to these brands? Is it how they speak? The logo design? What they stand for?
3. List the three things you would want your business to stand for, then select the one that best connects with your target audience.

FISAYO LONGE

Founder of Kai Collective

WHO IS FISAYO?

Fisayo is the founder of London-based, cult fashion brand Kai Collective. Her passion for fashion started through her fashion and travel blog, Mirror Me — since its founding, it evolved from a fun hobby into her full-time job— it provided her with opportunities to work and partner with big international brands like Google, Facebook, Lancôme and Nike, among others. After a few years in the blogging world, she now focuses on Kai Collective full time. In 2020 the brand became increasingly popular after being featured on Beyoncé's website as one of the Black-owned brands to support in 2020 to being featured on the cover of Elle's September issue.

FISAYO'S STORY

I've had my fashion and travel blog since January 2012. Whenever I would travel I'd go fabric shopping – I enjoy shopping for fabric, then I'd make clothes and people would ask me where I got the clothes from. This was how Kai Collective was born in 2016, based on the fact that people were asking for the outfits. That motivated me to start the brand. Initially I just wanted to focus on fashion, travel blogging and collaborating with brands, but to be honest I wasn't getting that many brand deals and I also wanted to do something that I had more creative control over. Something that I could just pour my heart into beyond a brief. I liked the idea of having a business and having more control over my career. I already had this community, or let's say audience — but I guess it was still a community, just not as close-knit as it is now.

I used to go to Durham University but in the summer of 2016 I got kicked out, so I didn't go back. My career, just being success-ful and making money, has always been my priority more than studying. I'm a smart girl. I do a lot of research, and I learn what I need to learn to do what I do — so that was my priority. I spent the whole year working on Kai; it had just started so it wasn't getting that many orders. And then I went to back to re-do my exams at uni the next summer. So I had a whole year, basically, to focus on my business and my personal brand.

The success of Kai has been because of the community. By the time I realised the importance of building a community, I had already built the community, so it wasn't something that I did consciously. Now I'm really aware of it. So, for example, I will go the extra mile in making sure that we're getting closer and foster-ing those relationships with our customers, because I've learned that community is everything, but it was only when it happened that I realised, 'Oh my god, this is important.'

Now that people feel more represented, the brand is getting more sales, and communication lines are open. I'm asking what they want in the brand, I'm asking for feedback, and the brand is *doing better. So it wasn't intentional – at first I was just sharing the journey of building Kai on my personal social channels. In hindsight, the brand would have done even better if I had focused on building a community from the beginning, but then again I like how organic it was because you can't really fake these things – or not really fake them, but you can't find them.*

Kai is a brand that has strong values around women, and sharing this came to me very naturally. *I didn't go to school for formal fashion training so for me it's always been more than the clothes. I love clothes and I love designing clothes, but for me it's more about the feeling, you know what they call 'brand'. I don't think that Kai would be as successful as it is, or at least starting to be, without the feeling that it gives women. I always knew that's how I wanted women to feel when they wore my clothes because that's how I like to feel when I wear clothes. And so the stuff that I liked wearing most was stuff that made me feel that way – powerful and in control.*

I would share my personal values on my social media channels. *I shared a lot of what I believe in, which sometimes doesn't always go very well, but I share it. I share what I think about women — having agency about their bodies, being naked if they want, showing their nipples if they want. Things that have gotten me in trouble over the years. And so it's just natural, that was just naturally going to go into my brand and the way we do shoots and the way we cast models and just the way we communicate — it's who I am. From the beginning I would attach tags to the clothing, I spoke about how I wanted women to feel — confident and sexy – in the clothes, because that has always been the most important thing.*

More recently I have started asking the community what they want to see. And it has changed everything. At first I thought a brand had to be very corporate and keep things undercover. I thought if we ask them what they want, then you look like you don't know what you're doing, especially because at many points I haven't really known what I was doing! So I thought that would be bad for the brand, but it wasn't. We have a segment on our Instagram stories called 'A Girl in Kai'. We like to spotlight customers and just ask them about things that are currently happening. So, for example, how do you feel about everything that's happened in the past few months with regards to Black Lives Matter? What principles do you live by? And then the final question is, would you like to share with us something you're working on at the moment? We then share that on our stories and profile one customer. This makes the women feel seen. And then weekly, we send out an email called 'Girls in Kai', where we showcase how different women have worn the brand — there is always so much to share, the community is strong.

At the beginning of the journey I used to run Kai by myself but now I have a team. The team has always focused on the newsletter, which has helped to build the community and increase sales — the brand has grown for many different factors but building this newsletter list was definitely one of them. I always look at the metrics, things like click-throughs, to see we are doing things right.

In the beginning when I launched the brand, I had a large social media following and still do, and I thought the launch would be very successful because of it. It was a bit of a shock when that didn't happen — it was very humbling. It wasn't the best. It was *difficult to deal with, but I learned a lot — it's not enough for an influencer to rely on their brand, especially if their audience is not engaged. At the time I thought I needed more followers and told myself 'It's because I only have 50,000 followers,' but then the realisation eventually came and I started to make gradual changes. At one point, I thought maybe the products were not good enough, or maybe they are not as cool as I think.*

Right now, I'm still very much the face of the brand but I don't plan to be for much longer. *When I hire people, I'm looking for women who are feminists. They don't have to be all the same things as me but they do have to believe in female empowerment – our values need to align. They just have to have this energy.*

Looking back, if I were to change anything, I would prepare myself mentally for how difficult it's going to be. *As I said, because I was an influencer (I hate that word), I thought that it would be an immediate success, and it was very difficult when it wasn't. It caused me to be depressed, and so mentally I just was not prepared for the difficulties of running a business and everything that comes with that. There were instances when shipment to customers would get lost, or literally not having any cash — I wasn't mentally prepared for entrepreneurship.*

FISAYO'S WORDS OF WISDOM

- Make sure that you are doing it for the right reasons — make sure you are doing it because it's something that you really believe in.

- Get familiar with branding and quality – understand the importance of good-quality product shots.
- Don't just try to do the same thing as someone else – be you and stay passionate.

@fisayolonge
@kaicollective
kaicollective.com

BRANDING YOUR SIDE HUSTLE

*'It's not what you think, but what they think that matters.
That is branding.'*

As covered in previous chapters, the brand is made up of the look and feel aspects, the identity. These elements make a business noticeable and make it stand out — how you'd identify someone by their voice, their touch and how they dress is the same way someone should recognise your brand.

Now that you've thought about the purpose, and why your side hustle idea exists, we now need to embed this into the look and feel of your product. Also, knowing who your customers are and their profiles (based on the research you've done) will help you create a brand that is aligned with them because, as I've been saying throughout this book, it is all about what your customers want.

The easiest way to approach this task is to think of your brand as a person and how they would express themselves to the world. When you understand the importance of how much this impacts if a customer shops with you and becomes loyal, then you'll consider taking this task seriously and making it a priority.

It really doesn't matter what type of side hustle you decide to start, this chapter is for everyone. Whether you run a charity, financial education platform or fashion brand, the following pages will guide you through creating the brand you want people to experience. It doesn't matter the size of your brand, every company can benefit from this kind of clarity.

Again, research is key here as you need to know what is already out there, so you don't become a spitting image of another brand, whether you knew them or not!

FEEL OF THE BRAND (INTERNAL IDENTITY)

We'll start with the internal identity of the brand because this is what dictates the external identity. For example, a brand that is likely to have a soft and friendly feel is unlikely to have a bold and loud logo, so leading from within is the best approach in order to get all things aligned.

An internal identity follows the same characteristics we use to label an individual; by having a clearly thought-out identity we are able to create a perception in the minds of customers. Read on to understand the important components of creating an internal identity.

HOW TO EXPRESS VALUES

Having your purpose in mind will help you decide on your values; these are the things that you stand for. Ideally, you want to list one to five values and you can decide to have this on your website and share them with customers as and when you feel it is necessary. But what you really want to do is find a way to express this through your marketing and actions — for example, deciding to give a certain amount of your profits to a cause, as this expresses what you stand for and that you are intentional in helping the world you are in.

Four ways to create brand values

- Brainstorm key words that represent the company you want to create.
- From the keywords select the top five important ones that not only matter to you but also to your potential customers.
- Share these with some people close to you and ask for feedback.
- Formalise these into written statements and express why your brand believes in these values.

Vision and purpose

As covered earlier, the purpose is the why you exist as a brand, and some brands tend to use this as opposed to having the traditional vision and mission statements, but they can still be helpful if you want to expand into the what and how.

Purpose = why your brand exists beyond financial gain.
Vision = the hope of what you want your company to achieve in lives of customers or the world through its purpose.

BRAND PERSONALITY

This is what customers relate to and interact with, the brand's personality — it is what you portray as 'who' you are. As I mentioned, think of your brand as a person. What personality would it have? Would it be bold and strong? Or confident and elegant? What you decide is what allows you to connect with your customers and who they want to connect with. Your personality should typically have three to five characteristics to describe it. *See diagram below.*

If your brand was a person, choose 3–5 words that would describe him or her[25]

Simple	Artistic	Strong
Beautiful	Bold	Childish
Funny	Serious	Goofy
Responsible	Professional	Angry
Dry	Corporate	Hipster
Wealthy	Sophisticated	Bohemian
Extravagant	Silly	Modest
Fun	Patriotic	Fashionable
Affordable	Rebellious	Activist
Charitable	Caring	Handy
Outdoorsy	Young	Effective
Reliable	Witty	Peaceful

---

[25] List courtesy of Shopify

Smart	Confident	Weird
Fast	Chill	Blunt
Manly	Experienced	Vigilant
Trendy	Flamboyant	Secure
Quirky	Honest	Rugged
Active	Bookworm	Sexy
Eloquent	Resourceful	Over-the-top
Expert	Efficient	Party animal
Energetic	Creative	Discreet
Daring	Zen	Exclusive

When I think about Tesco I tend to think good-quality and affordable, but when I think Waitrose I think top-quality, luxury shopping. These brands are targeting a certain type of person and as such have made sure their personality, packaging, shop design, etc., align with the feeling they'd like their customers to have.

BRAND TONE OF VOICE (TOV)

This looks at *how* your brand would communicate with its customers. What are the types of things it would say? Off the back of the brand's personality, you should be able to understand the brand's voice. This is extremely useful when you are considering communication such as social media captions, email marketing and even customer service – the things you say must be aligned so it seems like one voice. You should aim to be consistent with your TOV: you can't move from having a 'luxurious, sophisticated and reliable' type of tone to then being the 'party animal, weird and rebellious' brand. This needs to be consistent across all the touch points on which you communicate — we will talk more about this in the marketing section.

All these elements in the internal identity allow you to humanise your brand, which makes it much easier for customers to relate with.

BRAND MESSAGING

This can be defined as a set of key messages a brand uses to communicate its story and value to its target audience. It serves as a foundation to all the content, communications and marketing you would create for your brand. When creating the brand messages, you should keep your customer in mind — go back to your research notes and conversations with customers and think about what style of language would resonate with them: is it inspirational, witty or informative? Your messaging plays a key part in building a relationship with your customers and also driving sales. The TOV you developed will influence the way in which the messages are crafted.

To help you keep the messaging consistent, you should create a messaging template to go within your brand guide. Here is a list of things to include in the guide:

Brand promise: The value or experience your customer will receive from using your product.

Propositioning statement: A blurb explaining the value your audience will get from your product and how you will do this.

Target audience: Who they are; this serves as a reminder for who you are talking to.

Mission and purpose: What your brand hopes to accomplish.

Tone of voice: The way in which you would talk to your audience.

Elevator pitch: A quick 60-second pitch on how you would describe your brand.

Brand pillars: Three major themes, benefits or selling points that make your brand unique.

> **Headline benefits:** Short and punchy descriptions of your brand pillars.
>
> **Supporting examples:** How you deliver on the brand pillars/benefits.

And here is a working example for a video-conferencing software, adapted from a framework on www.pardot.com.

Brand promise: Easy video conferencing users will love.

Positioning statement: First video-conferencing product designed to connect individual employees and be fully integrated into every meeting room within a business.

Target audience: C-level executive (influencer), director of IT (buyer) and end-user (user/employee).

Mission and purpose: Our mission is to make every conversation face-to-face within a business.

Tone of voice: Empowering, progressive, human, simple and achievable.

Elevator pitch: A video-conferencing system that will connect every person and room in an organisation, bringing board-room video functionality to every device in a company.

Brand pillar: Easy

    Headline benefit: The system offers simple video confer-encing any employee can start or join with a single click.

    Supporting examples: Join calls from your calendar, SMS or email by clicking a URL; hand off video calls from your personal device to a meeting-room TV with a swipe or click; 5-min plug-and-play setup.

Brand pillar: Everywhere

    Headline benefit: Scalability allows 20 conference rooms for the price of one Cisco or Polycom system.

    Supporting examples: Comparable systems cost £10k per room; for the price of an iPad, the system can be deployed in every room; free apps to support stand-alone use from a desk or on the go.

Brand pillar: Enterprise

    Headline benefit: Designed as a business tool, not for social networking.

    Supporting examples: Must sign up with work email address, domain-based security model; built by estab-lished business-app developers to guarantee reliability and security.

Something to also note in the guide are words or phrases you don't want used in your brand messages. This guide should help you create consistent and memorable messaging across all your brand touchpoints.

LOOK OF THE BRAND (EXTERNAL IDENTITY)

Moving on to the external identity, which takes its lead from the internal identity, we will look at the visual components of your side hustle that will allow it to stand out. With this being the first thing people see, they are likely to create a perception of your brand in a few seconds, so you want to put your best foot forward and create a positive perception.

Logo

From the name to the look, a logo is powerful in attracting who you are trying to target. When thinking of the logo, think about how the name can help in explaining what your side hustle does. For example, Bookings.com, which gives away that it is about making bookings. The name could also be an expression of what you want to achieve, for example, take fashion brand 'Kai Collective'; in Nigerian 'kai' means wow.

Tagline

This is an opportunity to create a short memorable phrase of what you offer and the value you bring. I don't feel taglines hold as much relevancy as they used to, though, and some brands prefer to highlight their purpose statements and place this across all their brand touch points instead. Plus, nowadays the most memorable things are the experiences/feeling you leave with the customer and what you stand for; taglines can only take you so far — although Nike's 'Just Do It' will always be relevant!

Colour

Who remembers the era of 'millennial pink', the trendy pink colour that represented all things feminism and female? It was definitely a hit and represented more than just pink, although in reality it is just pink! Colours have a way of portraying information about your brand. Every year, 99designs.com share trends on colours, graphic design and website design. Check them out for some inspiration on where to start and, most importantly, think about what you represent and what colours have been associated with that. If you are a loud and confident brand then bold, bright colours are likely to work more than pastels.

Imagery

Imagery is just as important as copywriting, and you should be consistent with the images you portray across all your channels. For example, if you are a community-led sports brand you could show images reflecting members of your community as opposed to just products or stock images. Of course, in the early days you may not have much choice if no one has worn your products, but get creative and send samples to some potential customers and request they take natural, in-the-mirror shots. A brand that does this well is Never Fully Dressed.

There are also other elements that should be considered, such as IRL events; the experience you leave with the customer is a representation of your brand, from the venue, to how you manage the event, to the type of speakers you invite — these are all external elements of your brand that create a perception of who your brand is.

*

Your website and social media are brand touch points that use elements of both internal and external brand elements to engage with your audience.

Website

It is so easy to set up a website these days, there really is no excuse not to have one, even if it is just a holding page with a brief description. There are quick options via Wix, Squarespace and good old WordPress templates.

Your website gives you the opportunity to highlight all of the above things we have mentioned, from the internal and external elements: the 'about us' page, purpose statement, imagery and even how the website loads – all these things help in creating a perception.

Social media

When you first hear of a brand and want to find out more information about it, where do you go? For me, it's Instagram or Google. Knowing that customers will be hitting your social media channels on their first interaction with your side hustle means you should consider how you plan on portraying your brand digitally. Be consistent with colours, images and tone of voice in captions.

GETTING STARTED

Don't feel pressured after reading all of this. Giving your brand an identity is an important task but also a fun one, as you get to create a character. You can decide to do this yourself, co-create with your customers during the research and on social media, or you could reach out to a branding professional – it's totally up to you as to how you choose to invest in this process.

All of the above should be put into a brand guide that represents both your internal and external branding elements. This would typically be created by a designer but there are also templates on canva.com to help you do this yourself.

REBRANDS

Most times when people set out to do a rebrand it could be for several reasons, such as the brand not being aligned with its identity — so you've told people that you're a 'Beyoncé' but meanwhile you behave like a 'Britney Spears'. Both are great but customers expect you to live up to *who* you say you are. Or sometimes the behaviour of consumers changes, and as a result what they gravitate towards has changed too, and now the company wants to tell a new story.

Sometimes we make tweaks and not full overhauls. For example, with the rise and importance of sustainability, more and more companies are trying to make their brands not only sustainable but include this in their brand story as they know this is now an important value to their customers.

The point here is that there is always the option to make adjustments to your brand in the future if you need to.

GET TO WORK

1. List three examples of strong brand identities that you admire and what elements of the brand draw you in. Also list three brand identities you don't like and what elements about that brand you don't like.
2. What do you want people to think and feel when they hear your brand name or experience your brand?
3. List potential brand names that embody what you do and the feeling you expressed in the last question.
4. If your brand was a person, who would it be? What would their personality be like? List some of their characteristics.
5. List adjectives to describe your brand TOV, then begin to write a descriptive paragraph of what this voice sounds like.
6. Create some practice copy with your TOV in mind, something for your 'About us' page, social posts or website landing page.

GABBY EDLIN

Founder & CEO of Bloody Good Period

WHO IS GABBY?

Gabby Edlin is an activist campaigning for menstrual equity, and the founder and CEO of the charity Bloody Good Period. She was named as one of the Evening Standard's Progress 1000 Top Changemakers and Stylist's Woman of the Week.

Gabby has a Masters in Applied Imagination from Central St Martins, specialising in feminism and comedy. Before BGP, she worked in Arts Education for children and young people, and trained as an artist. She lives in North London.

Bloody Good Period now has a squad of over 700 volunteers, who provide more than 10,000 menstrual and hygiene products a month to people experiencing 'period poverty' across the UK.

GABBY'S STORY

I founded Bloody Good Period in October 2016. BGP got started because I was volunteering at a drop-in centre for asylum seekers and refugees with my local synagogue, and I realised they didn't have access to period products, so I decided I would supply them. I had read an article in Vice by Maya Oppenheim about what homeless women and people who menstruate do on their periods. The answer was it's a real struggle, and this stuck in my mind for a while. Very few people seemed to be having this conversation – and it was important. I started collecting period products after posting on Facebook, and it quickly grew beyond my friends and family, with people who I'd never met also sending me packs.

Pretty soon I had a light-bulb moment and started to think about branding what I was doing. I've always loved entrepreneurship, as I had several businesses in the past – I used to make jewellery and sell it at university, and I also had a greetings card business. It clicked that I could brand what I was doing rather than it just be 'Gabby is collecting pads'. Just to be clear, I'm not a particularly good designer, but I gave it a go anyway and designed the first pad logo myself. I felt it was important to get this branded so the business could become something bigger than me and not just an individual collecting period products.

There were no organisations speaking about periods the way I spoke about periods with my friends, which was without any stigma or embarrassment. I wanted the brand to reflect that, so I went for something bold, something that would stand out. I love the impact that design can have and I realised this is what was needed in this period-activist movement. I don't want the brand identity to take away from the work that we do, but it is crucial in the work that we do, as it ends the taboo and stigmas just by existing.

I wanted to see good design being coupled with activism, but we weren't comfortable with following how the big brands spoke about periods, which was in a stale and disempowering manner.

We then worked with a designer on the logo and website, which enabled other industries to support us and want to get involved. *It plays a big role in making us look like a professional and credible brand. Never underestimate the power of being 'cool' (I still can't say this with a straight face!). But really, I wanted this to be something people wanted to be a part of.*

The organisation grew from just collecting products, to people coming on as volunteers, to me bringing on trustees and trying to register it as a charity, with myself eventually being employed as the CEO. *This was essentially how it grew. I had never done this before, so I had no idea about funding it. A big part comes from public donations, and from individual sponsorships and trusts and foundations. We are a team of 12 now, which feels like the right amount for the team.*

A testament to our branding and work is that all partners have approached us to work with us. It's important that we attract and reach all types of people, which is why we do partnerships with brands such as gal-dem. *We did a partnership with the Body Shop, who supplied funding for specific education projects; these types of partnerships enable us to do the work we do. More recently we partnered with BrewDog to supply 'Bloody Good Beer' – all sales went towards BGP, and we used brand design to attract and tell the story of periods to the BrewDog community.*

My main goal is for BGP to not have to exist as an organisation – we are campaigning for the government to take this on.

GABBY'S WORDS OF WISDOM

- Create boundaries around your time and energy. It's impossible to work all the time, and you won't be able to do your best if you're burned out. The hustle is not 24/7.
- Write it down. Get to know reflective journalling. It will be so helpful for working through issues and celebrating wins, and it's a great log of everything you've done.
- Do good. Try to be ethical from the start in everything you do. You'll have to be your own moral compass, and it will be the most valuable tool you have.

@gabbyedlin
@bloodygoodperiod
bloodygoodperiod.com

FOUNDER AS A BRAND

'Consumers care about who is behind the brand.
Show them who you are.'

I've said many times throughout this book that your strength and advantage as someone starting a small business is that you have the ability to communicate directly and authentically with your customers as the founder. People buy from people, and nowadays they want to see the person behind a brand, not a faceless company. They are interested in what you stand for, your story, because your story gives them a reason to go out of their way to support you. This is the power of sharing your personal story or building a personal brand that leads back to your side hustle.

For example, Sarah Akwisombe, who I interview in this chapter, former blogger and now founder of No Bull Business School, has been consistent in sharing her story. Her story touches on how she was once broke, how her mindset was working against her and how she eventually transformed her life and money mindset. This story captivates her audience and gives them something to relate to, which drives them to buy her most successful course, 'Money manifestation'. Your story can play a big part in the success of your business.

Today we see those who have racked up social media followers, aka influencers, launch new businesses and create partnerships that allow them to have an extra stream of income or are their main stream of income. But you don't need to be an 'influencer' to achieve this; what gives them leverage is that they have been able to achieve the following things:

- They are clear on what they stand for and their community know this.
- They have established authority around a subject matter. This can be done in various ways; for example, if you are interested in beauty and review products consistently then it's likely you'll be a trusted source.
- Through establishing authority they have been able to influence and build trust with their community.
- Most importantly, they have a channel for direct engaged communication.

Being a person who has influence is not about the number of followers you have but about being a trusted source and voice. I personally believe this can help your business get off the ground in the early days, especially if you position yourself as the 'face of the brand' — something we may not all feel comfortable with.

This not only influences customers but can attract journalists, brands, investors, potential partners or employees that may be keeping an eye on what you are doing. I have always been very vocal about FWL in my personal brand. It's why the women in the community continue to engage because I humanise the brand and help it create a perception. Without FWL I would not have this book deal, my publisher would not have found me. Building a personal brand also creates you more opportunities.

*

My thoughts on personal branding supporting your side hustle were confirmed through a book I read, *Oversubscribed* by Daniel Priestley. He writes that in order to be a business that is 'oversubscribed' – aka selling out – there are three layers of branding that your business could take, and they are:

1. Product: The brands we associate with a product, when the company mainly focuses on product branding. For example, iPhone, Air Force ones, Jordans and Dior Saddle.
2. Company: The brands we associate with a company that are more concerned with the branding of their company. For example, Microsoft, *Vogue*, Coca-cola and Prada.
3. Personality: The brands we associate with people of influence who represent companies or brands. For example, Sophia Amoruso (Girl Boss), Anna Wintour (*Vogue*), Steve Jobs (Apple), Rhianna (FENTY) and Beyoncé (Ivy Park).

The world of branding has developed over the last couple of years from people caring about only the product to now wanting to know more about the company behind the product, and now we are in the era of people wanting to know about the person (founder/influencer) who represents the brand and what they themselves stand for. The personality brand is the most powerful of the three and will help drive growth for your business. If people can trust you, they will buy from you. Big brands use celebrities or influencers to add personality to their businesses, but here you have the opportunity to use your own voice and build influence.

I've mentioned the story of Away and Glossier so many times; do you know why? Because I have established trust with the founders through hearing their stories and their why on several platforms — this is what you want to replicate with your customers. Let's look at how we can do that.

HOW TO BUILD A PERSONAL BRAND THAT COMPLEMENTS YOUR SIDE HUSTLE

- Start as soon as possible and don't wait till you are launching your side hustle. It will make things much easier and allow you to be more authentic.
- Be clear on the messaging or story you want to create around your side hustle. Why did you start your brand? What matters to you? What are your core values? Why should we buy from you? Why should we trust you? Get clear on what you want to communicate.
- Decide on what you want to accomplish. Do you want to position yourself as a thought leader? Are you intentionally trying to raise awareness about your brand? Are you focused on building credibility? Or attracting a potential team?
- Determine who your target audience is.

- Choose the channels where you'd like to publish content and where you'd likely connect with your target audience, such as your own website, your brands channels, your LinkedIn, Instagram, Twitter, etc. (this is not about self-promotion but an avenue for you to talk about your brand in a way that is not 'salesy'). For example, if you are starting a personal finance educational platform, you'd need to build credibility. The best way to do this is position yourself as someone who knows what they are talking about, by either sharing valuable free educational content or even highlighting relevant experience and your qualifications. Your audience would want to know that you have the authority to start such a business.

- Choose the type of media you'll use. Video is very powerful these days and allows you to build trust much quicker than written words, but it's also not as simple to create. A mixture of both is nice.

- Build your audience; create engagement loops such as the option to comment on content or email you feedback.

MUST YOU BUILD A PERSONAL BRAND?

The question that is most probably lurking in your mind right now is do I have to be the face of my brand? Must I build a personal brand? Of course not, it's not mandatory, but it is an advantage in the early days of getting your idea off the ground and building trust with your customer. One day as I was aimlessly scrolling through Instagram (as we do) I came across

Kim Kardashian sporting her shapewear line, Skims. She was doing a short video tutorial on how to wear the backless shapewear dress whilst also sharing why she created it. Kim went on to share that she had loved wearing low-back dresses but always had to cut the shapewear in order to wear it under her dress which led her to creating Skims as there was nothing similar out there — more or less saying she is the only brand that does this. I was drawn in: there's nothing like someone being absolutely 100 per cent real with you and sharing their story of 'why' they started — it reinforces your message with existing customers, attracts 'lurkers' of the brand and will help in building a community.

If you're not comfortable with being the face, outsource this to influencers, but let's be honest, who has the budget for that in the early days?

While I strongly believe that founders should play a supporting role in their side hustle by being the face of the brand or building a personal brand, you must be cautious as anything you do will always be associated with the brand — and in a generation that hits the 'cancel' button without thought, it can be very hard to rectify when things go wrong.

GET TO WORK

1. Write down what your personal story is behind your side hustle.
2. Are you comfortable with being the face of your brand or building a personal brand? Journal your thoughts and understand where you stand on this.
3. If you'd like to be the face of your brand, what are you trying to achieve?
4. Create a piece of content that introduces your brand to the world in a personal way. Refer back to the first question to help you decide on what to include.
5. Once you have created this content, share with someone for feedback and, once finalised, share it with the world.

SARAH AKWISOMBE

Author, Founder of No Bull School & Boss Magic London

WHO IS SARAH AKWISOMBE?

Sarah Akwisombe is the South London 'no bullshit' Sunday Times bestselling author and founder. Her education business 'No Bull Business School' has thousands of female students who have gone on to create their own business empires and her new e-commerce business BO$$ MAGIC LDN brings a fresh new aesthetic to the mystical world, seamlessly blending spirituality and business.

SARAH'S STORY

I've always been involved in the creative industry; I started out as a producer and performer, then began a beauty agency with a friend but eventually landed on interior design. I knew absolutely nothing about interior design, which is why I started a blog to share what I was learning. I was planning on becoming an interior stylist and was documenting my own story of getting there and also the journey of renovating my own property. As my blog grew in popularity, a few brands reached out to me to contract me as an 'influencer' – mind you it wasn't called that at the time, it was just partnering with brands. This worked well alongside my full-time job; however, along the way I was fired and so I decided I was going to take the blog full time.

The transition happened quite naturally as I had the blog up and ready and I was able to make a career out of it. It wasn't common to have something like this, so everyone started asking questions around 'How do you do it?' and 'How did you build a personal brand?' No one in the UK was really talking about it and having known a lot about online courses because I had done them myself, and I was keeping an eye on what they were doing in the States, I decided to create a course: 'How I turned my blog into a business.' This was supposed to be a side hustle, an extra bit of income, but it actually took over what I was doing with the blog. I naturally transitioned into other topics such as growing your brand on Instagram. I basically teach what I've been learning in my life.

I personally think in this day and age it is almost necessary to have a strong personal brand to succeed as a business, but nothing is absolutely necessary. There are still a lot of brands being built without the personal element to it and they are doing well. However, having the layer of the personal brand allows you to achieve things much faster. For example, I knew nothing about interior design but the audience loved my personality and my approach to blogging – if I were a faceless brand, I may not have received that type of attraction. The same goes when I started teaching at No Bull

Business School: people loved my style and no-bull advice, which is what has led to our success – plus, there was no one out there like me doing it. This grabbed people's attention; people buy into who you are in order to buy into your business. Some of my clients don't like taking this approach with their business and I tell them that's fine but they'll have to be realistic with their expectations – it will move slower without the personal branding layer.

Being the face of the brand can be tricky. If you are the face and you fall out of favour with the public you could easily start losing customers, and you need to be aware of this. Have it in the mix of other marketing strategies, use it to leverage but don't use it as the only strategy. In instances where I've fallen out of favour – I don't sell – but with my second business, Boss Magic, I rarely use the personal branding strategy so I know it's a business that can survive without me.

Both the brands I have built I have done so on purpose, but I have made sure to have a balance with also focusing on sales. You need to have a balance of purpose and sales – there are some brands that are fully focused on sales and going into this next generation of business, and I can predict that they won't do well. People are more woke in their consumer choices, but equally if you're too far with the purpose then the focus is not on growth and sales and that can create cash-flow problems. Communicate your purpose and have this across your social points but don't forget about sales – if you don't have sales you won't be able to fulfil your purpose. They are not mutually exclusive.

SARAH'S WORDS OF WISDOM

- Get really clear on what exactly you stand for as the face of the brand. It must be clear and concise.
- You must brace yourself for those that don't agree with what you do and don't stand for.
- Remember that it's okay to grow and change your opinions – brands and people evolve. Talk through those changes with your community, bring them in on the journey of your evolution.

@sarahakwisombe
@nobullschool
sarahakwisombe.com
nobullbusinessschool.com

GETTING YOUR FIRST CUSTOMERS

Every day new ideas and businesses come into the world. As you are reading this, someone somewhere is launching a business — the majority go unseen and unheard because the founders have not understood the concept of sales and marketing. They assume 'if I build it, they will come' but it's absurd to think that a business could succeed without having a good sales and marketing approach. On the other hand, some businesses thrive from day one, knocking close to £100k in sales in less than a year. Sometimes this is down to luck, but most times it's a good brand with a killer marketing and sales strategy, whether it be organic or paid — they become the 'it' brand that everyone wants to associate with. An interesting fact: they don't always have the best product or a marketing budget, but they know how to connect with their target audience.

With the emergence of the internet, everyone having access to a mobile device and social media platforms, you can now market and sell your products online and reach countless customers in seconds. In order to succeed at both marketing and sales, it is necessary to understand the psychology of your customers' buying decisions, why they buy from you, what it is that they want to see from you in order to encourage them to click the 'pay' button. Is this an emotional purchase or a logical one? You should by now have a good sense of what type of messaging they'll be drawn to based on your research and conversations with them. This chapter will help you learn how to connect with your customers and get your first couple of sales.

A simple formula we are going to use to help get your business out there is below; this is also the same formula you can use when launching a new product or service in for an existing business.

AWARENESS

Building awareness around your brand and yourself is the first step in getting your idea out there into the world. Consumers respond positively to stories, so you must raise awareness in a way that is focused on telling a story and not just shouting about a product. At this stage, you may not even have a product but you do have a story.

Psychologists believe that if you can create an emotional connection with your audience based on your story then you are on the way to having them as a customer. One of the greatest ways to do this is by initially being the face of your brand.

No matter what you are selling, you are selling a story first. Your story should help build a rapport and spark an emotional response. When telling the story of your brand, you should be focused on the why behind your business and you can start sharing this before your product or service is available. When you read the stories of the women I have profiled in this book, the majority of them first created awareness around their brand and built a community before they had officially launched their business.

WAYS TO CREATE AWARENESS

- Use PR to share your story with the media (see page 255 for this).
- Share your story on social media. I'd also share the behind-the-scenes process of starting your business. People are curious and want to support a small business.
- Collaborations with similar brands or communities can help you spread the word about what is to come beyond your own audience.

BUILD COMMUNITY

Once you have created awareness, you want to be able to attract that audience to become part of your community. A community is defined as a group of people with similar interests, needs or problems. Community hasn't always been a focus for businesses, as previously people were more concerned with just attracting an audience, but the latter does not help to retain customers and move them through the full cycle. Communities don't just like your product, they like you and what you stand for. At this stage you want to be focusing on them and not you, giving them valuable content that can support why they have decided to join your brand community.

When growing a community, focus on engagement and not the amount of people following you; it's pretty useless if you have a community of 1,000 but only two to three actually engage – a business owner's worst problem. Your focus must be on engagement over numbers.

WAYS TO CREATE A COMMUNITY

- Create a mailing list – a list of potential customers' details given to you by themselves. You can use this mailing list to send them useful updates about your brand.
- Join social network groups – people want to belong and share their interests. How can you create a two-way dialogue for this? You could try using Facebook groups, Clubhouse or even Slack.

- Create useful educational content around your business or the interests of your community.
- Host IRL or online face-to-face events to engage and meet with your community, and give yourself the opportunity to get to know them better.

RE-ENGAGING THE COMMUNITY

Perhaps you have a community that exists but you have not been communicating with them because your business was put on hold. During the pandemic many businesses were affected in this way, but now that the world is opening up again, it is important to start to re-engage. Here are a few things you could try:

- Communicate why you were silent.
- Share what they should expect from your business.
- Remind them why they joined your community.
- Move on as normal, don't focus too much on your absence but continue to engage.

PROMOTION

Promotion is essentially marketing, sharing your brand messages and creating awareness about your products. Marketing has the power to tell your story effectively. To increase sales tremendously. To build tribes that are loyal.

To create fomo (fear of missing out) even when there is truly nothing to miss out on. Often the goal is to increase sales, but that is not always the objective; these days customers expect you to build a relationship with them before making a sale.

The promotion should happen way before the actual launch of your business, especially for a new business, as it takes about seven times for a customer to see something before they purchase – this is called the power of seven. Never get tired of promoting your business – you need to be unforgettable.

Make sure that all your promotion is aligned, keep the messaging consistent, and for more impact, promote at the same time on different channels. For example, once you send out an email promoting your product, start promoting on social media and any additional channels you use.

Fail to plan, plan to fail — you know the drill.

WAYS TO PROMOTE

- Showcase samples of your products.
- Use creative ways to talk about the value your brand brings.
- Pre launch day, inform your email list that 'something is coming', then on launch day make sure to inform them first.
- Ask your customers to make pre-orders of your product by placing a deposit or purchasing it in full before the launch day. This allows you to gauge how many people are inter-ested in your product.
- Use influencers to help generate buzz. The great thing about using an influencer is that they already have an engaged

following and can do the heavy lifting for you. They can choose to work with you for a fee or accept gifts in place of payment — building a relationship with these influencers is key to getting them on board. Make sure they are aligned with your audience as it won't be helpful partnering with an influencer who shares content on a completely different subject area or different niche. For example, if you are launching a kids' fashion brand, sending your products to an influencer who focuses on fashion but has no kids would not be effective. If you then send to an influencer who focuses on fashion and has kids this would appear more authentic, and she has the audience who is interested.

- Tap into social media advertising. Facebook, Pinterest and Instagram are the most affordable but in the early days try them all out and find out what platform performs the best for your product. You can choose to restrict these ads to your current followers or include identical followers too — make sure to use ads that are engaging.

These things build excitement around your brand and help to provide you with an educated audience willing to buy on launch day.

Just before my book deal came along, I was preparing to launch an online course I had created for those who want to start a side hustle. I began by promoting this via a series of social media posts discussing the things that hold people back from starting a side hustle. I would direct people to sign up to the waiting list so they would know when it launched.

All your marketing should be solution-focused, referring back to pain points they are solving. During the promotional period make sure you direct customers to where they can actually be met with a sales message, such as your website.

SALES

In order to sell effectively to your customers, let's look at the psychology of buying, as this will give you a clearer picture of what drives your customers.

Psychologists believe that every person is pursuing one of these three life pillars:

1. Wealth
2. Health
3. Relationships

We all have one if not all of these pillars high on our agenda; as a brand you need to understand where you fit in with them. For FWL, we would fit in under wealth as we provide knowledge, tools and resources that can lead to women generating wealth for themselves. This is what my customer is looking for. You want to start a side hustle, but I'm confident you also want to create a wealth of income for yourself.

Once you have discovered which one your customer is looking for, let your sales focus on how you can help them attain one of those life pillars – in a subtle manner. Speak to the needs of your customers.

HOW TO DRIVE SALES

- Do it yourself. No matter what you are selling you have the ability to sell it yourself. Whether it is software or a fashion brand, get in the face of your customers yourself and sell to them.
- Always give clear calls to actions when selling to customers.
- Identify common objections/obstacles and address them in your sales message/descriptor with the value it delivers. For example, if you sell virtual assistant services to entrepreneurs and a common objection is 'your prices are too expensive', your response shouldn't be about price but about the value. For instance, your sales message could be: 'We help you save more time so you can focus on the things that bring your business money.'
- Scarcity – no one likes fomo (fear of missing out), so if you can create some sense of urgency and exclusivity this tends to drive people to take action.
- Social proof – this can be evidence of something you have created for yourself as a result of your product. This could also include before and after pictures telling a story about your product.

RETENTION

At this stage it is all about retaining those new customers who have bought from you. You should be acquiring new customers often, but you should be equally concerned about retaining the existing ones; both are important. For those you manage to retain, it is a demonstration of their loyalty. Research has found that if 5 per cent of customers are retained this can lead to 25–95 per cent increase in profit — this allows you to spend less on marketing as it is quite expensive to continue to acquire new customers.

HOW TO RETAIN CUSTOMERS

- Create trust: it's the easiest thing to lose and the hardest thing to gain back. Gain trust by continuing to offer consistent great quality and value. A survey by InMoment showed that customers hold longer relationships with brands they trust and from whom they know what to expect despite there being cheaper alternatives on the market.

- Provide great customer service; when customers complain, be timely in your responses and show genuine care.

- Reward repeat customers via loyalty programmes or discounts.

- Create targeted email campaigns to give customers early access to new products, discounts or sales.

- Invite them for special events or contact them directly for their views on existing or new products — this makes customers feel special.

- Create educational content that demonstrates how to use your products/services.

- Reshare user-generated content. Customers like to be recognised, and if they create content that includes your brand, share it, as this is free marketing for you.

ADVOCACY

If all you do is find one loyal customer, that is one more promised customer and a marketer who you aren't even paying. Advocates are those that sing your praises and spread your business through word of mouth. When customers become fans they start selling your own product for you, to family and friends and beyond. Not all customers will get to this stage, but the goal is to try to convert as many customers into advocates as possible.

HOW TO BUILD ADVOCATES

- Affiliate marketing offers advocates the opportunity to make a fee from promoting your products or services to their friends and family.
- Introduce brand ambassador programmes.
- Give good service over and over again, and keep it consistent. This breeds trust and even when you can't keep up with the service, explain why.
- Be transparent with your customers, let them know when changes are being made or when new products are being developed. Don't just share the good stuff, share the not-so-good stuff too.

USING THE INTERNET TO GROW YOUR BUSINESS

The most affordable way to reach your customers is through the internet, giving you access to a global audience. As of January 2021, there were 4.66 billion people around the world using the internet. This is an opportunity for you to reach customers beyond your family and friends and boost your brand visibility. Below are a few ways you can use the internet to grow your business and attract customers.

SOCIAL MEDIA MARKETING

Out of the 4.66 billion people using the internet, 4.2 billion people are using social media, which also will continue to grow – your business having a presence on social media is a no-brainer. As I have mentioned before, when I first hear of a brand I immediately go to Instagram to search for their page. This gives the initial impression of the business, which is why it is key to have good valuable content on your pages and, of course, a clear call to action.

Social media marketing can be both organic and paid, and in the early days you want to focus on organic reach until you are clear on your target audience. Once you are clear, you can target your customers with paid social media marketing, which gives you more value for your money and allows you to save time, as you are focusing specifically on customers and eliminating unnecessary marketing efforts.

To avoid overwhelm, you should consider only using one or two platforms in the beginning. You should test which best work for you and where you are getting the best engagement for your customers by using the platforms' inbuilt analytical tools to understand how your followers are engaging. Do also look at trends to understand what social media platforms your target audience most engages with and to also understand the new features that could support your marketing.

Your demographic should be a deciding factor when thinking about where to market your brand. For example, if you are trying to reach Gen Z then Facebook is not the place, rather Instagram and Tik Tok. You could also look into what your competitors are using and what has worked for them.

Here are eight social media channels to start with:

INSTAGRAM

Regardless of whether you have a product or service-based brand, Instagram is a place for high-quality visual content as it is a mobile, visual app. Its most popular type of content is Instagram stories, which I would utilise to drive conversations through creating engaging content such as polls and opening up the DMs for communication. Make sure to use hashtags on grid posts, which helps in discovering your brand.

FACEBOOK

This platform encourages all types of content including traditional text, images and videos, as well as Live Videos and

Stories. Facebook also offers groups – unlike the other channels – which allows you to create a community and build closer relationships with your customers.

PINTEREST

This is great if you have a product-based brand, because just like Instagram it is all based on visuals. Each Pin could be an image, infographic or video, and link back to your website. When I would create articles for FWL, Pinterest was a great marketing platform as I would use strong cover images to promote the content that would drive traffic back to the website.

TWITTER

A place to drive conversation around industry topics, share your brand's POV, engage with customers and get feedback. Twitter limits each tweet to 280 characters, so your message has to be precise. They have also recently introduced Twitter stories and Spaces, which allows you to host live audio-only chat rooms. This is another perfect opportunity to get closer to your customers and grow your community.

LINKEDIN

This is brilliant if you have a B2B model and are targeting companies, certain decision makers within companies and those in professional corporate jobs. LinkedIn has evolved from the stale résumé platform to being more 'social'. Users are now just as personal as they would be on other social platforms. Hubspot found that LinkedIn was a leading platform when it came to generating new business leads.

YOUTUBE

While shorter videos are more appropriate on Instagram, this is a great platform to share a series of longer video content, if that works for your product.

CLUBHOUSE

A great platform to draw closer to your customers and have 1:1 conversations. Giving customers access to you makes them feel closer to the brand.

TIKTOK

A place to create short, viral, entertaining pieces of video content that last around 15–60 seconds each.

EMAIL

Out of all the options on the internet to market, email should be your priority and you should be growing your list from day one. An email list allows you to own your customers' data, whereas with social media the platform owns the data. If the platform crashes or you lose your social media account, all the data is gone, but with an email list, it is yours until they unsubscribe. Use every opportunity possible to drive customers to sign up to your email list.

You can use email not just for selling products but also for sharing valuable content with your customers. A regular newsletter is a tactic you can use to stay connected with your customers and keep them informed on new products. Make sure to never spam them, though.

WEBSITE

Your website is the ultimate opportunity to market your brand and you can leverage other platforms to drive customers there. Here are a few helpful tips for your website.

ABOUT US PAGE

This is your opportunity to make a strong impression on your customers and to highlight why you exist as a brand and why they should shop with you. Keep this page concise but informative.

SEO MARKETING

This is 'search engine optimisation', which allows you to use methods that help in placing you in a good position in search engines such as Google. It will require you to use specific key words in your content on your website, giving you more of a chance to appear high up in a search engine when specific words are searched for. This is an important marketing tool, especially if most of your customers use a search engine to look for the type of products you are selling. Tools that can help in understanding popular keywords are BuzzSumo, Google Ads Keyword planner, Google trends and Moz.

ANALYTICS

Use analytics to understand your customers' behaviour, what pages they are visiting the most, where they are coming to your site from, how long they are spending on each page, why they may be abandoning a cart and how you can create a better shopping experience for them.

SPEED OF WEBSITE

If the speed of your website is slow, this will affect how you rank in the Google search engine, as they want to give their users the best experience and they will rank a user-friendly website high up. A slow website will also mean customers dropping off in frustration. There are plenty of online tools that can help you check your speed regularly.

CLEAR CALL TO ACTION

Regardless of the platform you are using, the goal is to grow your business by attracting new customers and keeping the existing ones engaged. On all your platforms you must make sure to give your audience clear calls to action that tell them what to do. For example, if your objective is to grow your online audience, a call to action could be: 'Share our post with a friend,' or: 'Click the link and subscribe to our newsletter.' You must always be clear what action you want your audience to take, be consistent and don't feel like you are constantly repeating yourself. With all the brands online, there is another brand fighting for your customer's attention.

UNDERSTANDING A CUSTOMER'S JOURNEY

The diagram below shows the customer's journey and the potential touchpoints at the different stages of the journey — touchpoints are the different ways in which your customer could interact with your brand and receive your message. This is important for you to know, so you can strategically map out the journey and how you want the customer to 'find you', make a purchase and then become a brand advocate.

GET TO WORK

1. Brainstorm the ways in which you could create awareness about your brand before launch day. Think of the most effective ways and the most affordable, too.
2. List influencers in your industry that you could potentially partner with to promote your business.
3. What brands or communities have a similar customer base to yours? How can you tap into this? What type of partnership could you create?
4. What could a potential loyalty programme look like for your brand?
5. What type of content would be most suitable for your brand? Is this what customers would want?
6. How can you share your personal story with customers across social media?
7. Which three social media channels could you start with?

EVA GOICOCHEA

Founder of maude

WHO IS EVA GOICOCHEA?

After studying marketing in New York, Éva returned to California and spent her early career as a legislative aide in healthcare at the California Medical Association. She then went on to work in e-commerce and brand strategy with companies including The Natural Resources Defense Council, ADIDAS Y-3 and SLVR, Squarespace, Steven Alan and Josie Maran Cosmetics, an organic beauty brand.

In 2012, she joined the early team at Everlane, where she solely built out their social media, culture and talent strategies. In 2015, she co-founded her first company, Tinker Watches, with her husband Ian and designer Luke Ragno.

That same year, she converged her passion for healthcare and brand to begin the development for maude, a modern sexual well-ness company built to challenge a legacy industry and serve the customer through quality, simplicity and inclusivity.

Since its launch in April 2018, maude has been featured in Vogue, the New York Times, Fast Company and some other 600+ publications. In July of 2019, maude was one of CircleUp's

25, an 'annual award recognizing some of the most innovative consumer brands on the market' and has been heralded as 'redefining the sex essentials industry for modern consumers' by Forbes.

EVA'S STORY

I studied advertising and marketing and had worked as a legislative aide in healthcare and then in marketing for brands, but where I really learned to cut my teeth and get to grips with startups was in my role at Everlane. This is where I really understood how to build a brand and product. I left there in 2013 and started building maude. I've now been working on maude for six years and we have been launched for about three – I worked on it for two years before we launched, I made all the mistakes, didn't go to business school, so I was very much a newbie.

The idea for maude came about from a conversation that happened between me and the co-founders of a small watch company we started. The conversation was 'Why has nobody taken up this actual wellness space, modernised it and made it easily approachable?' This was a lunchtime chat and in that moment I realised this was the idea I'd been waiting for. I started to pursue it; no one was really interested but I dropped everything and knew it was something I had to do. Everything I had experienced up to this point made me ready to start maude. The biggest lesson was recognising sometimes it will just randomly come to you.

When I got the idea, the first thing I did was put up a website, but I had been building websites and brand guides for a while. It's not necessarily the first thing you should do as it's not a fully baked idea, but this was something I chose to do.

The first year was about talking to people and validating the idea — I believe it's absolutely critical for people to do it earlier on. Know the market and talk to people. Do surveys, focus groups — it synthesises your thesis and you are really able to justify whether the idea could work, or it may go the other way and, based on the conversations, you realise it won't work. It's important that you do this before you jump and spend money to do anything else. From here I worked on the brand book (see below), but this evolved over time: the brand as it is now didn't fully take shape until two years later and it's gone through a couple of iterations.

We were working with the factories directly but it did take a long time to find the right one for us. We worked with a different factory for every product. If you're launching a beauty brand, you could definitely stick with one factory to make all your products, but in our category each specialises in something and it takes a long time working with factories to innovate.

About a year before we launched, we had started working on our PR. We reached out to the media to share our story and asked them if they would want to cover it. During this time we sent out a survey which was filled out by 650 people — ranging in age from 19 to 81 – and 98 per cent of them said the same thing: 'It's uncomfortable to buy these products,' 'It's misogynistic,' and 'It's outdated.' All of this helped in validating and crystallising the idea. We told the survey participants that we would send them the product after they filled out the survey (they didn't see the product but they knew they were going to get something). These were the first people to try our brand. In terms of how we were able to get 650 participants, I emailed everyone I knew and asked them to share with 20 friends – that was our experience.

I have made all the mistakes you're not supposed to make but what really helped was an entrepreneurial programme I did in New York. I also took a course at Harvard called the Entrepreneurial Essentials, which walked me through the entire journey of entrepreneurship and the basics. If I had taken this earlier I would have made fewer mistakes — I really recommend taking courses or trying to learn before you start.

When thinking about redefining an industry or category, as we did with maude, I really encourage people to think about the universal pain points you are going to solve, finding your space, and really knowing your audience. Our challenge was how to build an inclusive company when you're asked to focus on one audience first. It may be discouraging to start because you see a saturated industry, but again, I would say find your audience, stick to your thesis, and start.

In terms of funding the idea, I raised three rounds of funding, which was a little tough. The first round of a fundraise is about selling the fact that there's a market, the idea and also selling you as a person – it's all about the belief in you. For the second round, once you've already taken your product to market, it's truly about the numbers – you have to be careful here because if you launch with no money to market the product and try to raise it after, your numbers are very unlikely to be something to write home about. It's definitely not easy to get funding but just something to think about if you ever plan to raise. What investors are looking for in the first round is for you to know your costs of goods, your unit of economics, how much you're going to spend on marketing, how long it will take you to get to a certain milestone and how that money is going to be used on operations. It's really all about the business model and being clear as to where the money is going — you'll need to get your sh*t together. It won't be good enough to just have a 'good idea' – and remember to stick to the plan and timeline you have given them.

Touching on business plans, we didn't really have one, but we had a financial model built from as early as possible. I would align with someone that can build a really strong model — this will help you guarantee that you know how to get from a to b.

EVA'S WORDS OF WISDOM

- If you don't have a background in business, take a business course. Not only are you learning the basics but you're also learning the language and half the time the challenge is not having this knowledge.
- Really find someone who can help you create a financial model so you can use real numbers and understand where you are going.

- The value of a brand is so important, so create a brand book – this will help cement who you are so you will stop second-guessing yourself. This is what you would use to work with freelancers and photographers and also just help you know your brand and messaging – it doesn't have to be excessive, it could be just 10 pages. This would include visuals, how you speak, what your brand is and what you stand for. It's an exercise in making choices and sticking to them.

@evagoicochea
@getmaude
getmaude.com

GETTING YOUR SIDE HUSTLE KNOWN

'You can create people's reality by influencing their perception – own the narrative.'

When you have a goal to reach an audience and you have little to no budget for marketing, what can help you get your brand known is PR and word of mouth. Securing media coverage is much easier than it was in the earlier days as we now have easier access to journalists and influencers, and these days with the fight for audiences everyone is looking for a good story to tell. Every time a story goes out about your brand it gives you the opportunity to create a perception, to own the narrative. PR is a brilliant strategy to tell a story but it's important to remember that it is part of the broader marketing plan and should be used alongside other tactics. In this chapter we will look at when and how to go about publicising your brand and the effective ways to do it. One piece of good coverage could change the face of your brand forever.

There are three types of media:

Owned: This means that you own the media, you have control of it and it lives on your channels, such as via a newsletter, website and social media channels. This should not be an afterthought, as the way customers usually first interact with a brand is through their owned media.

Earned: This is the tactic that appears more authentic and authoritative as it is others writing about your brand. Traditionally you'd pitch to a journalist and they could choose to feature you in a story or write an article on your brand. It is also the hardest type of media to gain, as journalists are inundated with requests daily, so the most important thing here is to build relationships with the right people.

Paid: This says what it is, paid PR which could be through advertising and allows you to be more targeted in reaching your audience. Here you'd pay to advertise your *owned* content or even the *earned*. Sponsored posts in publications are also a form of advertising.

Types of press and media coverage:

- Podcast interview
- TV interview
- Feature in a magazine
- Mention in an article
- Product/service placement in a roundup recommendation
- Radio interview
- Sponsored post

Media coverage has the power to:

- Build brand awareness
- Attract potential customers
- Help with recruiting
- Generate new leads
- Attract investors

- Position your brand as a thought leader
- Help increase sales (although this is a byproduct of PR and not what PR focuses on)
- Position your brand high up in search engines

PITCH IT

There is some sense of pride that comes with saying: 'I was approached by the press.' Who cares? These things can't always be organic and the truth is there is so much noise these days that it's really hard to get recognised. When it came to featuring women in this book there were so many options, it was hard to choose, so now think about how hard a journalist may find selecting which brands to write about. Pitching gives you the opportunity to get into the face of the reporter, build a relationship and sell yourself, whether it be an article, or for TV or radio interviews. Below is a quick plan on how to be more strategic with your pitching and press coverage.

I have only pitched twice for For Working Ladies and on both occasions I received press coverage, one of those publications being *Forbes*. I had been following the journalist's writing for a while; she focused on women at work and female founders. One day I sent her an email introducing myself, what I do and if she ever needed access to female founders for comments I could make an introduction. I invited her to an event I was attending as I wanted to meet her and see how we could potentially work together on other projects I had lined up. A few weeks after meeting, she wrote an article about 'female founder communities to watch' and For Working Ladies was included. Pitching is all about relationship building.

So what's stopping you from pitching your brand?

PLAN IT OUT

Before you approach journalists, make sure you have a clear plan about what you want to achieve with your press coverage.

Objective

What is the goal here? Be very specific about what you are trying to achieve. Things don't always have to be sales-related, you may decide to focus on building the profile of the founder or positioning your brand as a thought leader. Whatever it is, make sure you get clear on this as this will help you with the next point.

What's the story?

Not all stories are press-worthy. Based on your objectives, what type of story can you create that would interest readers but more importantly the media? Stories with a hook, that may catch people's attention or inform them about something new that ties in with their interests. These are the stories the media want, something to attract their audience, listeners or readers. For example, Daye, a femtech brand, is likely to approach either a health- or female-focused publication to share their story behind why they created the first tampon infused with hemp. This is information that would interest media outlets and readers.

If you are trying to build your profile as a founder, what is so interesting about you in relation to the brand? Why would anyone be interested in your story? Think about what makes you unique. Again, create a hook so compelling that people would want to showcase your story, and make sure you tie it back to your marketing message. Alternatively, you could offer yourself as a thought leader on industry topics and be willing to comment on relevant topics.

Be targeted

Once you have decided on the angle of the story, be targeted in your approach with the media outlets. Make sure the media has an interest in the type of story you are sharing and their readers are your potential target audience. If you sell luxury watches and they usually showcase lower-end affordable products from Primark, is this the right fit? Are you really targeting your audience?

PRESS KIT

A press kit includes information about the company and also brand assets such as high-res images, FAQs, showreels and previous press interviews. Always have this ready in case the media reaches out to you. This kit will help them have a brief overview of what you do.

GET THE TIMING RIGHT

Securing media coverage is an opportunity to reach a wider audience, an audience that you don't have. You have to get the timing right in order for it to bring the returns: should you be approaching the press on launch day? Or before? Or after you've perfected your product, have good reviews and enough supply in the instance that customers come rushing for your products. It all depends on your goal; if you are looking for your first set of customers it might mean getting press to help build your waiting list or build your community. You may be focused on press in order to announce a new feature or added product. Whichever the case, the objective determines the timing.

CALENDAR OF EVENTS

Create a calendar highlighting significant days that your brand could tie into a story for the press. For example, going back to Daye, approaching the press just before International Women's Month is a good opportunity for them to pitch a piece on women's health, then journalists could write an educative piece on this topic.

HOW TO CONNECT WITH JOURNALISTS

As mentioned, this industry is all about relationships. Even if you hire an agency it will need to have a relationship with the media they intend on pitching to. Take time to research the journalists/reporters, see what topics they are interested in, how often they publish. You can do this in a variety of ways:

#JournoRequest: A hashtag used mainly on Twitter by journalists looking for stories to write or comments from experts or the public. You can follow this hashtag on Twitter so you don't miss the opportunities.

Social media: You can connect with journalists and editors on social platforms such as Instagram or Twitter, pop them a message introducing yourself and referencing a piece of work of theirs that you like, but I'd advise sending them an email if they are not responsive in the DMs.

Print magazines: Look at the masthead, this is where they list all the departments and who works for them. Contact the editor, managing editor or features editor for pitches.

Online publications: In Google or LinkedIn, search 'digital editor' or 'managing editor' plus the publication name; if you don't find an email address, use a tool such as ContactOut when in their LinkedIn page, as this will help retrieve it.

DO IT YOURSELF – WHEN YOU CAN

When it comes to pitching, it's always best in the beginning for founders to do this themselves — from my own experience, journalists like hearing from you and feel more of a personal connection to your story, which they don't always get from speaking with a publicist on your behalf.

VISUALS SPEAK LOUDER

Beyond sharing a release with a media outlet, catch their attention by also sharing high-quality images or videos of your product, event or promotion which could be useful footage for TV producers. This is your media kit.

GO NICHE

In the beginning you may not be able to secure national coverage in the top-tier publications, but you could try going for the small, niche publications in your industry. The great thing about small and niche is that engagement tends to be much higher, so you are likely to get readers to take action. Think of blogs, community newsletters, podcasts or magazines, Facebook groups or Instagram lives.

GIVE THEM AN EXPERIENCE

Whether you have a product or service, how can you give the journalist an experience of your brand? This may mean sending them the product you sell or giving them a trial of your service/ product. Whatever it is, journalists like to write authentic stories on their experience with a brand rather than just report the brand's existence.

SHARE, SHARE, SHARE

When you get featured, make sure to share it widely as this will allow more people to discover who you are and want to feature you on other platforms.

FIVE STEPS TO TAKE WHEN MAKING THE PITCH

1. Introduce yourself. Give a quick summary of what you do and why you are connecting.
2. Reference the journalist's/reporter's work and why you decided to contact them over other journalists.
3. Attach important assets such as a compelling press release, product images or videos.
4. Include a call to action.
5. Follow up!

MEASURE SUCCESS

This part is important because it helps you evaluate if your objectives are being met and if your PR tactics are working. You can measure PR through various ways depending on your objective; for example, if your objective was to increase the signups to your waiting list, check the amount you had before press then monitor the growth after – did you get the results you wanted? If not, why? What could you do differently? These are the types of questions you need to ask. PR is not about fame but a tool to be used for actual business growth.

GET TO WORK

1. Look through the media outlets your audience likes and start compiling a list of the reporters that would want to cover your side hustle. Keep their details in an Excel sheet.
2. What are your objectives with getting press?
3. When would be the right timing for you to secure press?
4. What story would you be interested in sharing with the press?
5. Is that story relevant to your objective?

JAIME SCHMIDT

**Founder of Schmidt's Naturals,
Investor @ Color Invests and
Author of *Supermaker***

WHO IS JAIME SCHMIDT?

Jaime Schmidt is an entrepreneur and the founder of Schmidt's Naturals, a brand of natural personal care products that she started in her kitchen in Portland, Oregon, in 2010. Jaime is known for modernising natural personal care products, including the customer-favourite deodorant, and bringing them to the mainstream market. Under her leadership, Schmidt's grew into a household name lining the shelves of retailers including Target, Costco, Whole Foods, Walmart and CVS across 30 countries. In 2017, Schmidt's partnered with CPG giant Unilever, with Jaime continuing as the brand's founder.

Today, Jaime is focusing her efforts on helping emerging entrepreneurs pursue their own dreams. Jaime is the co-founder of Color, an investment portfolio that supports women and people of color. Last spring, Jaime launched the Entrepreneurial Dream Project, a grant fund and mentorship programme that supports early stage entrepreneurs impacted by the recent economic recession. Recipients receive capital and coaching from a dream team of 50 business leaders, from Mark Cuban to Rebecca Minkoff and execs from Adidas to Harry's.

Jaime recently released her first book entitled **Supermaker: Crafting Business on Your Own Terms,** *a personalised guide on how to put your business on the map, turning your passion into profit.*

JAIME'S STORY

I had gone to college for an undergraduate degree in business. *I chose this because I didn't quite know what else to do and it made sense as a practical degree. After I graduated, I found myself looking for a job. I settled into human resources. I was working for a staffing company and made my way up. It didn't take long before I really found myself in a comfortable job working at a prestigious foundation in downtown Chicago. The pay was great and the benefits were amazing, but I just wasn't loving the work and was turned off by the thought that I might have to do this for my entire life. I made a commitment to myself to keep exploring. I didn't really know what that looked like and so I went on to get another degree. This time, I got a masters in Sociology, and my thinking there was, 'I still didn't know what I would do with it but at least it's a step towards something a little more meaningful.'*

After this, I moved to Portland, Oregon. *The West was really intriguing to me because people were really creative and I loved all of the nature and outdoor living it had to offer. But when I got here I felt like I wanted to fit into the city, everybody was creative and pursuing* *something – they were artists and musicians. It made me think, 'What's my calling? What can I do? What can be my thing here?' And so it was kind of this combination of, one, trying to find myself with my paid work and my career; then secondly, trying to find just a little side hobby to keep me excited and to be meaningful in the city.*

When I moved, I remained in human resources at a public school system and decided that I have one year to work in this job. *If I haven't figured out meaningful work yet, then quit, and spend some time getting your hands dirty — I followed through on that promise. I had a little bit of money saved up – not a ton but enough to spend a few months sort of exploring and getting my hands dirty and trying all sorts of things. I did some interior design, took some sewing classes and was brewing kombuchas – just trying to make new things. But when I really discovered something that I loved was when I took a class on how to make shampoo. I happened to be pregnant at the time and just found myself in this class. I had this huge belly and was falling in love with what I was doing. It made sense for me, too, because I wanted to use healthy products while pregnant because everything you put on your skin gets absorbed into your bloodstream, and so that was another motivation.*

I had not really recognised the business potential of creating natural products, but was just enjoying it as a creative outlet. *But then I realised in Portland, there are a lot of places to sell, such as farmers' markets and street festivals — you just set up a table and you're good to go. So I brought my products to the market, and I realised there was a real business opportunity with what I was doing because people were telling me that my natural deodorant product was really* *incredible and it had changed their lives. They had found a natural deodorant that worked — I realised that the market needed something like this because there were a couple of other natural deodorant brands on the market at the time, but they had a reputation for being ineffective and bland with their scents and packaging. I knew there was an opportunity to shake that up and do something a little more innovative.*

So I decided to go all in and I still maintained a couple of little side hustles in the earlier years. *But then once I really felt like I was on my feet, I gave up those little side jobs and then I put myself 100 per cent into Schmidt's and then, as I mentioned, you know, never anticipating it growing to the scale that it did but just through customer word of mouth and distribution, it did.*

I had a tiny little house that was about 750 square feet, which was where I had started creating our first products. *I was newly married. I was a new mum, and while my son was napping I'd be in the kitchen, making products, tiptoeing around trying not to wake him and, you know, most new mums are napping alongside their baby because we're exhausted, right, but I was just so excited and inspired by what I was doing, so I was just using that time to work.*

We had this unique way of standing out. The branding at the time was a lot different than what we were seeing on the shelves. *A lot of the other products were a little more cliché with a predictable aesthetic. I wanted to do something more colourful and modern. So that was really important to me. And also, the fragrances that I was using, those didn't exist yet. I wanted something that caught* *people's attention. We had this community of customers that were just so passionate about the brand and what we were doing and really believed in my founding story. I think that was a part that was really interesting to people – that it was born in a kitchen, that there was a mum behind the business, that I had just started this as a hobby and so I think that people were just inspired by that and liked supporting that kind of business.*

We really caught the attention of some of these brands, like Unilever, for example, who later on acquired us. *They have many other brands but noticed that we were taking from the market share. A great example is when we launched with Target, our sales were so tremendous and they noticed this. They could have tried to replicate the product but what they could never really do is create the brand equity that we had built up and this loyal customer base and so it made sense for them to acquire us. So they reached out and then we got a broker on board and when that happened we had a couple of other strategic firms that were interested in acquiring Schmidt's. We had several on the table at once and were having conversations with all of them, and then later on Unilever was the clear winner. It was what made the most sense for the brand.*

JAIME'S WORDS OF WISDOM

- Say yes now, then figure out how. This will unlock opportunities and force you to learn as you go.

- Avoid a rigid business plan. It's important to leave room to adapt and evolve.
- Persistence pays off every time. Show unrelenting belief in what you're doing, and others will too.

@jaimeschmidt
@schmidtsnaturals
@colorinvests
schmidts.com

4

THE IMPORTANT STUFF

From legals, to accounting, to learning how to get funding for your side hustle, this part covers the important stuff – yes, boring, but important. I encourage you to read this section through before you take any action to start your side hustle and get in contact with the necessary professionals who can help set you up for success. There are a few businesses that require legal checks before they can go live, you'll need contracts between you and your co-founder so there's no confusion along the way and you'll need to decide if you're setting up as a sole trader or limited company — there is a lot to consider.

This information is not financial or legal advice, so do get professional advice before proceeding!

LET'S TALK LEGALS

*'This topic may be a bore but
it's better to be clued up now rather than later.'*

How I wish I had known most of this topic when I decided to turn FWL into a business, the painful experience of setting up a limited company and not understanding the importance of accounts or if a limited company was even the best route for me. I've now experienced it all – been employed, a sole trader and had a limited company. There is so much to be aware of before taking any decisions — I get it, you're excited and want to get your idea of the ground immediately, but slow down and get protected before you make a move that could cost you, like literally CO$T YOU. The advice will obviously vary depending on the type of business you set up but I'll try to cover as much as possible. However, do seek professional advice, and in this case professional legal advice, wherever necessary.

REGISTERING YOUR BUSINESS

How you go about registering your business will determine how you can operate and will help you avoid any trouble with tax regulations – all of this can take less than a week. There are mainly two options for those with a side hustle: sole trader or limited company. In the UK when you are starting your business you will need to contact Companies House and/or HM Revenue & Customs (HMRC), in the US it's slightly more complicated as depending on where you operate taxes, etc., will change. Either way, you'll need to register with both state and local governments.

Before you decide to register your business, do check if the name is already taken at Companies House, as a domain and on socials — if not, secure it immediately, then go ahead and register it; this will avoid making any changes in the future. You've got better things to worry about.

Below I'll go into detail about the business structures.

SOLE TRADER

This is the simplest business structure of the lot and the most appropriate if the income is generally low. With this structure, you'll often be referred to as self-employed although it really just means that you are trading as yourself, under your own name in most cases or with a trading name. If you decide to take this route, you will own all the assets and despite being called a sole trader you can employ people.

You can have a full-time job and be self-employed at the same time — there are no laws around the amount of work you can do or how much you can earn. If you decide to go for this option you will only need to register with HMRC as self-employed and submit an annual self-assessment, which will determine how much tax and National Insurance you pay. FYI, if you fail to do this, as mentioned above, it will cost you, as this could result in fines and interest on late payments (I know a bit about that!). Most importantly, remember to always keep records of your business sales, invoices and expenses — don't throw these out!

Please do seek advice from an accountant. I personally have gone the limited company route based on advice from my accountant around my earnings — this is really not black and white and advice is needed.

Advantages

- You keep all the profits.
- Very little paperwork to be done as you only have to file your accounts once a year.
- There is more privacy as your information cannot be located online as it can with a limited company.
- Any losses incurred can be offset against your full-time income.
- Tax-free opportunities for those with a side hustle – I'd suggest speaking with an accountant about these, though.

Disadvantages

- Although you are registered as a sole trader, your business name is not registered so it is not protected as it would be as a limited company. However, you can protect it as a trademark.

- You have to file taxes yourself and it's not automatically done as it is when you are employed.
- Personal assets will be at risk if your business runs into trouble. You are liable for the debts and liabilities of the business.
- You cannot take equity funding as an option as there are no shares.

LIMITED COMPANY

When you set up a limited company you will need to register this at Companies House and also choose an available name — this will be viewable by the public, making all information such as account filings and directors viewable. All limited companies must have a director who is over 16 years of age and also a shareholder — a shareholder can also be a director, which means you. If you choose to go this route the company will be taxed on its profits; as with a sole trader, you will need to let HMRC know.

Advantages

- You can claim back business expenses.
- The company is liable for any debts, not the founders.

Disadvantages

- Current appointments and filing history are publicly registered and accessible at Companies House.

- It takes more time compared to a sole trader as there are more legal responsibilities and administration tasks to look after.

VAT (VALUE ADDED TAX)

It is only compulsory to register for tax if your turnover exceeds a specific threshold in a 12-month period; this is £85,000 as of 2020. VAT may be beneficial to you if you are selling to other VAT organisations, as they may be able to claim VAT back from HRMC.

CHECK YOUR CONTRACT

When starting out your business as a side hustle, do check that your contract at work allows you to earn extra income and there are no internal policies around side hustles, especially if there is a conflict of interest. Your employment is important, so make sure to protect that. If there are no policies then it is up to you if you want to share your side hustle with your employer.

BUSINESS INSURANCE

Whether or not you are legally required to have business insurance really depends on the type of business that you have. If you employ staff then the only mandatory insurance is employers' liability cover; again, depending on the nature of your business, this may change. It's important that you get clued up on the insurance you'll need based on your industry, as avoiding this could bring problems.

REGULATIONS/LICENCES

Depending on the industry you are in there will be certain regulations and licences that you will need to have. This not only protects your customer but also you and the industry as a whole.

PROTECTING YOUR BRAND

Here I'll share how you can legally protect your brand from other brands using or copying your work, logo or even brand identity.

TRADEMARK

Your logo and business name can be protected by registering it as a trademark – basically anything that you use to make your brand distinct from others, such as symbols, a letter, taglines or figures. This essentially means that if anyone uses these items you are protected and have the right to contest. To register your trademark in the UK, you need to first check that no one has trademarked the same name or brand. You can do this through the Intellectual Property Office in the UK.

COPYRIGHT

This allows you to protect your work and gives you the right to say how and who can use your work – this could be quotes or images. Under UK law your work is automatically copyrighted the moment it is created and in fixed material, so there is no need for registration.

In the early days when writing articles on our website, I would source images from the internet (like we all do!), sometimes images from Instagram, Pinterest and anywhere online that had great images — of course, I would add the source link unless it's from an image bank and there is no need. One day I received an email saying I had been fined £250 because I used an image from someone's website without their consent. I mentioned that the image had been referenced but they made it clear on their website that images are copyrighted and should not be used. However, I found this image on Pinterest and so missed this — I immediately took the image down and the mistake was excused. Be careful when you use other people's images, especially in the early days when you do not have original produced content.

PATENTS

A patent is a legal right granted by the UK Intellectual Property Office for a new invention — this allows you, the patentee, to take legal action against anyone that uses this invention without your permission. To apply for a UK patent, you can do this with the UK Intellectual Property Office. If the patent is granted, which usually happens about four years after the application, then you'll have rights for 20 years from the date of the application. If you decide not to use the invention you could license it and allow others to use it or even sell it on. Do further research on this as there are a few criteria for you to meet if you'd like to patent your invention.[26]

IDEAS

Sorry to burst your bubble but ideas cannot be protected as they are not deemed intellectual property like patents, designs, trademarks or copyrights. However, you can use NDAs to protect your conversations.

NDA (NON-DISCLOSURE AGREEMENT)

Non-disclosure agreements can help protect your company's confidential information and intellectual property when shared, as anyone who signs the document is legally bound to not divulge any of the details you have given them. These can be used in several situations, such as sharing your idea with someone, speaking with investors or when working with contractors or employees. If you plan on getting advice from people and fear them running off with your ideas, I'd advise that you look into using an NDA — it can be awkward at times but very necessary that you protect your valuable business

---

[26] https://www.mewburn.com/law-practice-library/uk-patents-the-basics

information. When I hired a freelance content creator, I made sure she signed an NDA as she would have access to information that could put FWL at harm. Which takes me to my next point.

USE CONTRACTS

Regardless of how small you may be as a business, when engaging someone, always use contracts. It can be helpful to keep templates that can be quickly amended when need be. These contracts make clear the terms in which you are working with someone and not only protect your rights but theirs too.

GET TO WORK

1. What business structure would be best for your business? List the advantages and disadvantages of choosing this business structure for your side hustle.
2. Make sure to register your business name and logo as trademarks if you plan to use them exclusively.
3. Are there any regulations or licences that you need to be made aware before you start trading?

RACHAEL CORSON

Co-founder of Afrocenchix

WHO IS RACHAEL CORSON?

Rachael Corson was 19 when she co-founded Afrocenchix, an award-winning ethical startup that creates safe, effective, vegan certified products for Afro and curly hair. After graduating with a Law degree from the University of Birmingham, Rachael studied at the Institute of Trichologists, then later graduated from UCL with an MSc in Medical Anthropology (with a dissertation completed at the University of Cambridge Medical School).

As a public speaker, Rachael is best known for her winning business pitch to celebrity judges including P. Diddy, Gary Vee, Vanessa Kingori (publishing director at British Vogue) and Ashton Kutcher at the WeWork Creator Awards, two days before giving birth!

Rachael lives in London with her teacher husband and two young children. When she's not raising her babies or leading a creative and diverse team towards huge, global goals at Afrocenchix, Rachael plays the guitar, runs, bakes and writes sci-fi.

RACHAEL's STORY

I met my co-founder, Joycelyn, at university in 2008. I was studying law and she was studying sociology. She was the other black girl in halls! Although Birmingham as a city is multicultural, the University of Birmingham is largely white and middle-class. We bonded at a night out and quickly became friends. We would talk a lot about hair because at the time I couldn't afford to go to the hairdresser and her sister is a hairstylist so Joycelyn had some experience, and used to relax my hair. One day she said she's not doing this any more because it isn't healthy for my hair as I had bad eczema and other conditions. I initially had no interest in natural hair. I like my hair to look nice but I didn't have the time to invest in it. Joycelyn was more into hair than I was. I saw natural hair as really high-maintenance and something I didn't have time for.

We ended up talking about natural hair products because she had been experimenting with products to help her grow back her edges.

Joycelyn gave me some oil that she had made for my skin. I was super excited as I wasn't allergic to it and my friends used to joke I was allergic to everything. I tried to get Joycelyn to turn it into a business, as there were many people like us who were experiencing the same thing and needed natural solutions. Joycelyn immediately said no because she didn't go to university to start a business. I said fine, I'll help you put some money together so we can do some research, come up with a formulation that works well and sell the excess. This was the entire plan: we would help some people and cover our costs – we often had schemes like this. There was a time we noticed the guys in the halls were always spending money on ordering pizza for dinner. So we asked them to just bring all the ingredients to cook a meal and we would do it for them and end up with a full kitchen cupboard. They got a good meal for less than the price of a pizza and we had our food shopping provided! We were also on a society committee together. So running small schemes or projects wasn't new to us, we had so many we had done in the past – we were always looking for a new hustle.

When we started this business, we set up a really basic website just to share information with people, as we had done our research through visiting the library and reading cosmetic science journals and looking into the chemical makeup of different ingredients. The research came before this was even a business. We were research-ing to make sure what we were creating was going to solve our problems. After doing the research we ordered raw materials and worked on getting the measurements right, so that we could create products for ourselves for our skin and hair that would get us through university. We put £50 in each and ended up with 100 skin and hair oils. We kept some and sold some at a market store. We then entered a business innovation competition and won some money. They said if we registered the business they would give us more money — for them that was a sign we were taking it seri-ously. This was the point at which we registered the business, in 2010.

We were both university students during this time; we had full-time degrees and also part-time jobs. When we left, I got a job at

Mondelez head office while Joycelyn was finishing her degree, but we lived together at this point. We raised £10,000 in Angel investment for Afrocenchix. Some of that money went to appointments and some of that money went to stock, then the rest of it paid for me to study trichology: the science of scalp and hair. We had still been running this as a side hustle as it didn't yet make sense to be running it full-time. We had a lot to learn and a long way to go in terms of developing the product; at this point it was still pretty much R&D. The products we have now were first launched in 2014.

The more research we did, *the more we would blog about what we had learned and our customers would tell us about their stories, the more we realised we couldn't stop there because one: what products would we use, and two: what products would our customers use? I would read up more and more about women's health and the equalities there were and wanted to solve the threat to health and wellbeing of black women. We shouldn't have to risk our health in order to look attractive and for our hair to be more manageable. I knew this wasn't acceptable.*

We wanted the business to be big. *We had a huge mission and we wanted every under-served customer to be able to access safe, effective, ethical cosmetics. In order to do that we would have to build a huge global business, and that's what we're working on now.*

In 2013 we were still side hustling but it was becoming rather unsustainable. *Joycelyn was coming to my house after work and we were making around six bottles of shampoo in our kitchen a night, and Joycelyn would post them out the next day. We were having to do this three or four times a week. We had no lives, it was* just work. At this point, I decided to quit my job, applied for a scholarship at UCL and ended up doing a masters.

UCL had a good support system for entrepreneurs, so we got involved with some university entrepreneurship programmes and received more funding. With that money, we were able to improve our website, bring out new products and start thinking more seriously about being in the business full-time. At this point Joycelyn had gone part-time at work and I was a student. We really wanted to go full-time but couldn't because it was not generating enough money for us to pay ourselves a salary as we chose to reinvest the profits for growth.

In 2016 Joycelyn quit her job completely, so she went full-time. At that point I had graduated and was working as a student business advisor in UCL for three days a week and the rest of the week working on Afrocenchix. During this time we learned about venture capital investing and different ways to finance a growing business, and we created a strategy and business plan.

The pivotal year for us was 2017, when we moved our website from WordPress WooCommerce to a Shopify store, and overnight our sales tripled, simply because we no longer had website glitches and bugs. On our previous website, people were trying to buy products and couldn't, carts were being abandoned, they were phoning us for help, everything was a mess! So moving over to a better CMS we were able to instantly improve our sales. At this time, I had just given birth, was working two contracting jobs and tutoring. Me and Joycelyn were not paying ourselves yet, but we had a brilliant first employee who massively helped with growth.

In the same year, we put together a pitch deck and decided to raise investment and began pitching. We set out to raise £350,000 but raised over £500,000 in 2018 ... but it took a while. The money came in in 2019, and we were able to hire a team; we went from a team of four of us to having eight full-time employees on payroll, including me and Joycelyn and some additional contractors too.

Our sales are now over 10 times what they were before we raised investment. In the last 10 years, eight black women have raised venture capital in the UK. There weren't really opportunities before now and they still really aren't for black women – less than 0.03 per cent of VC financing goes to black women. But black women are more likely to have a business or a venture than their white counterparts. There is clearly an issue in the venture capital world. Despite this, we have made our peace with these stats and have continued to do our best.

We have been part of several accelerator programmes and have been passed over for financial support but instead given shiny awards. We are constantly told that our pitch was the best and fantastic but only end up with awards. No money. We have seen time and time again our white male counterparts raise investment for their business and one year later decide to move on to something else. This is very common in venture capital.

One of the things that set us apart is our robust product development. We formulate the products ourselves. Me and Joycelyn do the bulk of this work: she took a soap-making course and as mentioned before, I studied trichology — we also work with various cosmetic scientists. In our industry most things are white-labelled or made in people's kitchens – the white-labelled products are made following all the laws and regulations and are quite a high standard. The things made in people's kitchens are often not safe because they've not been tested. The barrier to entry into this industry is quite high due to the EU cosmetic regulations changing in 2012. It's important that you follow the regulations around skin and hair products, not just because it's illegal if you don't, but also because it's important that you create safe products.

At the moment, the law requires you to put your products through three levels of safety checks at a minimum. We've mentored or advised several people in this industry and discovered that they have not completed safety assessments. It takes a while, at least six months for the basic tests, but it's necessary to keep the industry safe. In order for our products to get into Whole Foods we needed to have had all these assessments done. A lot of small natural hair brands can't trade in high street stores because they don't have the documentation to prove they are trading these products legally. We do a lot of education around this to help up-and-coming founders and to keep our community safe.

RACHAEL'S WORDS OF WISDOM

- Do your research, do your research and do your research.
- Rest and look after yourself; there's no joy in working late nights and not eating well – you can't give from an empty cup.

- Make sure you're solving a real problem and continue to keep up the research to keep confirming you are solving the problem in the right way. The best businesses are the ones that are solving major problems for people.

@raecorson
@afrocenchix
afrocenchix.com

HOW WILL YOU FUND IT?

'Money is oxygen and every business needs it to exist.'

Besides lack of time and resources, another obstacle in getting a side hustle up and running is access to the funds that will help — will you take external money or will you completely fund it yourself? There is no wrong or right answer, to be honest. This is something that should be well thought out before taking action: once external funds come into your business, you must be accountable to those who have invested and I've heard it's a pretty big task. How you are held accountable varies depending on who you have taken investment from — it also puts you in a position of being in debt or giving away equity.

With all the funding information given in this section, please do your research, consult professionals and understand what you are getting into.

WHY WOULD YOU WANT TO TAKE EXTERNAL FUNDING?

There are several reasons why people consider this option, including needing money so you and the team can work full-time on the business, getting the first couple of customers, taking the idea from MVP to actual product or needing to cover legal fees. The reasons vary.

HOW MUCH WILL YOU NEED?

How much you need will dictate where you may go to seek financial support; the same applies to the type of business you have. For example, if you expect to raise finance from venture capitalists later, you should start by setting up a limited company. All of this will determine the options available to you, so it is best to seek financial advice before making such important decisions. In whichever case, before considering taking external support, you should create a plan to map out how much money you will need and how long it will cover you for.

YOUR FUNDING OPTIONS

Bootstrap

To bootstrap means the founder of the business uses their own personal money from their pocket or resources to support their business. Typically what happens here is when the business makes its first couple of sales the money is reinvested back into the business — this is the most popular approach. According to research undertaken by funding broker the Company Warehouse in 2016, 56 per cent of these startups were using their own money to entirely fund their business while 82 per cent were using self-funding as a significant part of their funding mix.[27] The benefit of this approach is that you have total control and do not have to give up any of your company's equity. A few popular self-funded businesses are Spanx by Sara Blakely and House of CB by Conna Walker — two female-founded businesses that are both global and doing significantly well.

Friends and family

Borrowing from friends and family is another popular source of funding, although this option can create a tricky relationship if the plan and agreement terms are not clear. When requesting money, make it clear in writing what your terms are and if you plan to pay back, keep everything in writing and discuss it with them so there is no room for confusion.

Grant schemes

This is a brilliant option as they are free, so they do not need to be paid back; however, they are hard to find, which makes them competitive with eligibility depending on a whole range of factors. Grants are given by the government, or public and private bodies; to find ones appropriate to your business, google them, ask other business owners and do your research.

---

[27] www.thecompanywarehouse.co.uk/blog/bootstrapping-preferred-funding-model-for-startups

Crowdfunding

This is another popular option, when you allow a crowd of individuals to contribute to your business idea. Women who have opted for this option tend to get great results, as research says they are said to be great storytellers. I would highly recommend the book *The Crowdsourceress* by Alex Daly, a crowdfunding consultant who has helped many businesses raise finance through this route — you can read her story on forworkingladies.com.

There are three types of crowdfunding:

- Reward/donation crowdfunding: Here you reward donors with a sample of your product or another incentive like being recognised on their website, or a gift if they give a certain amount.
- Debt crowdfunding/peer-to-peer lending: You receive a loan from crowdfunders and then repay it.
- Equity crowdfunding: You receive money in exchange for giving out equity or shares.

Crowdfunding sites to check out:

- Kickstarter
- Crowdfunder
- Natwestbackherbusiness.co.uk
- Seedrs
- Crowdcube
- Funding Circle
- Patreon (not really crowdfunding but good for creators to collect funds from supporters)

Before using these sites, make sure to do your research about the companies.

Bank

You can go to the bank for various options, such as credit cards, loans or overdraft.

Startup loans

These loans may require you to meet certain criteria for you to apply but they are as good as bank loans. However, they typically come with some sort of support, which is often an essential part of the service, especially if you have little experience. A popular one is Virgin Start loans and startuploans.co.uk. but do research and seek advice to see if these are right for you.

Accelerators

Startup accelerators support early stage, growth-driven companies through education, mentorship and financing. Startups enter accelerators for a fixed period of time, and as part of a cohort of companies.[28] Most accelerators will give you an investment once the accelerator programme is finished in return for equity in your business; this will differ with each accelerator.

---

[28] https://hbr.org/2016/03/what-startup-accelerators-really-do#:~:text=What%20 are%20startup%20accelerators%3F,of%20a%20cohort%20of%20companies.

Accelerators to apply for include:

- Y Combinator
- Techstars
- Seedcamp
- Entrepreneur First
- Founders Factory

Angel investment

Angel investors are individuals (generally high net worth) who invest their own money in an entrepreneurial company in exchange for shares in that company (equity). These can be people in normal everyday jobs willing to invest in companies they believe in. Angel investors tend to invest at the early stage (pre-seed and seed) of a company, specifically in the idea phase or when the company has its first initial customers. Just like previous options mentioned above, these individuals can offer more than money by also sharing their expertise to support your business. If you decide to go with this option, do find out more about the Enterprise Investment Scheme, which could help your investor with tax relief.

Where to find angel investors

They could really be right under your nose, which is why when you are looking for them, you should tell everyone about your idea – it could be your colleague.

Sites to check out include:

- Angelinvestmentnetwork.co.uk
- LinkedIn Angel investment groups

And if you are interested in learning about how to invest in startups, a good friend of mine, Andy Ayim, runs the angelinvestingschool.com, an online course in which you can learn the basics of how to get started with investing in startups.

Venture capital

This is capital that is usually invested in businesses that have high growth potential. People who make these investments are called venture capitalists. They are not the same as angel investors, as it is not their money and they are investing on behalf of organisations that they have raised from, such as pension funds, financial firms or insurance companies.

PITCHING YOUR IDEA

Whether you're pitching for a loan from your parents, to the bank, investors or donors, your pitch should include the following:

- The story of why your idea needs to exist: the problem and solution.

- The market: customer, competition and USP – how you plan or are currently marketing and reaching customers.
- The team that will be running your business.
- What you will be spending the funds on.
- Projections of your financial year.

THE HARD TRUTH

For women, these options are limited, especially if you decide you want to reach for the stars and apply for VC funding — all female-founder teams are far less likely to get investment from VCs than their male counterparts, with these statistics being worse for women of colour. It's good to note that many of these decision-makers who make up 91 per cent of these committees are men, as several such funds have been set up specifically for women in order to level the playing field. Examples of such funds are Backstage Capital, Jane VC and Female Founders Fund.

As I mentioned in the MVP section, the amount of money you have the ability to raise does not determine success for your business and is a vanity metric.

There are more options on lending which I have not mentioned here. Do make sure to seek advice from a financial advisor in order to make a sound decision for your business.

GET TO WORK

1. How much will you need to kickstart your side hustle? You can understand this through forecasting and budgeting.
2. Can you bootstrap this business?
3. If you need extra support, list the friends and family members you could potentially reach out to.
4. If you need a larger amount to get started, what route could you see yourself taking?

FIONA KOLADE

Influencer & Digital Entrepreneur

WHO IS FIONA KOLADE?

Fiona Kolade is a full-time influencer and entrepreneur who helps influencers learn how to create value-driven content and land partnerships with dream brands. Fiona moved from the corporate world to pursue entrepreneurship full time and loves sharing her journey with her female community. She is a wife, mother and believer – passionate about showing women that they CAN live a life and have a business and home that they love.

FIONA'S STORY

My journey really started off with me as a blogger, before I really embraced the title of influencer and what that means now. I was really passionate about hair care and learned from a friend of my sister that what I was doing to my hair was not necessarily in favour of its health – like the ultimate health that would allow for me, for example, to grow thicker hair, or not necessarily thicker but to have fuller hair, and longer hair. And so I embarked on this healthy hair journey and just documented it on a blog at the time called Love Your Tresses. And that's when the journey began, brands started to *reach out. More than that, I started to see, essentially, a commu-nity of women who, like myself, wanted to really look after their hair in a different way to perhaps what we were exposed to growing up and I guess 'bad hair practices'. At that time, the natural hair movement in the UK was really picking up. Of course, typically, things are done first of all in the US, and so the natural hair move-ment was picking up a lot faster there.*

As I grew, and the community was growing, opportunities came. *At this time I was in a full-time job – I was in the financial world as an analyst. And I think essentially what happened was I just got really passionate about this hobby. I loved to see the community, and the opportunities that were arising were really exciting. And at the same time, to be quite honest, the job that I went into post university was not necessarily something I was passionate about, it was something that was what my parents really wanted me to do. I was good at maths and economics and the role just made sense, it was a well-paid job, and I had the skills needed to do it. What happened was, as I found, I was loving what I was doing on the side, I really understood that the job I was doing professionally was not what brought me much fulfilment. Don't get me wrong, I loved the company culture and had amazing colleagues but didn't feel it was a career I wanted to pursue in the long run. So I decided to leave my job prematurely, which is really where this is going and what I want to get at. I left my job prematurely, thinking that being able to monetise the hobby that I had would be an easy ride, because I kind of knew some people were able to do it. And then the learning curve began. I was out of work for eight months. And in a nutshell, during that time, the money I thought would come in, did not. I was earning peanuts. And when I say peanuts, I mean, I* don't even think I could afford to take us to McDonald's a couple of times a week. I was not earning anything close to what I was bringing in from my corporate salary.

We dipped into our savings for our first house, as we were renting at the time. We were using all of that money to essentially make up for the money I wasn't bringing in and hubby was so supportive. But there came a time when it was just like, we are not the type of couple that wants to live without intention. We want to build a legacy. Are my actions currently aligned with where we're trying to go as a family? No, they're not. So I sat down with hubby to create a plan, which involved me going back to work, and as God would have it, I managed to land a job that paid even more within two weeks of applying for roles.

I had an advantage, which was that I'm a language speaker, I speak German. So every role I've done in the corporate world has been a German-speaking one. So that definitely did play a huge part in it. I went back to the corporate world and I had a game plan with regards to how long I was going to be there. I worked my corporate job during the day and would create content at night and over the weekend. I was filming, I was recording, I was investing in resources to ensure that the next time I would try to leave my job things would be different.

I stayed in my job for a year, and within that time the opportunities that I was working so hard to be able to get started to come to fruition, and I experienced my first five-figure brand partnership. This was huge because at the time I didn't have what many people would see as a huge social media following. With regards to that five-figure partnership, at that time, that was not a conversation that was being had in the social-media-influencer world amongst my peers. This was a big deal. I had friends who had 10 times or even more of my following who had yet to experience this, so that really opened me up to the potential of this industry and this career path, and I soon went on to quit my job and go at this full time.

This lasted for a year, before I had to go back to work again, but this wasn't really to do with me not earning enough. I hadn't quite matched my corporate salary, but we were doing well. The actual reason was because we wanted to buy a house; we were in a position to buy but I didn't have enough tax history as a sole trader, so I went back to work to help with this, and then the funniest thing happened: I got pregnant! Hello, plot twist.

Instead of returning back to business after we bought our home I stayed with my employer. Due to being so sick during most of my pregnancy, the job security proved to be a blessing in disguise vs being in the early stages of running a business.

With regards to the transition between the second time and now, I also started to introduce my own digital products. Suddenly, it was not just about being an influencer but more about how well you monetise and leverage what you're currently doing. For example, I introduced a hair ebook. It was a very low-ticket hair ebook but it helped me to understand the value of my expertise at the time and packaging that into something that would not only serve people but also serve me. I then went on to launch my very first online course, 'The Influencer Game Plan', to help aspiring *influencers learn how to build their brands and monetise more consistently. The main difference this time around was also investing in my craft more than ever.*

One of the key things that helped sustain my business *when I left the corporate world the final time was financial planning and forecasting. I didn't want a situation where I would leave my job and then have the experience I did from the first time where the money wasn't coming in. It's something that I tell people they need to do if you're going into business, which is all about, you know, determining what that end income needs to be for you, factoring in things such as your rent and whatever expenses that you have, as well as what you would like to pay yourself, whilst making sure that you're being reasonable – of course, bearing in mind that this is your first go at it. Ask yourself, how many, for example, core sales do you need to make and how many brand partnerships do you need to have? So that's what I did; it was about having a financial goal. You need to have something that you're working towards.*

FIONA'S WORDS OF WISDOM

- Invest in your growth. Freebie university will only take you so far. You have to invest to see a return, not the other way round.
- Make data-driven decisions. The numbers do not lie. Intuition and gut feelings are not enough when running a successful business. Back these with data and metrics

and use this to inform your next steps and marketing efforts.

- Listen to your audience! Your greatest asset, especially if playing in an oversaturated marketplace, is how well you know your audience. Take the time to know them on as granular a level as possible.

@itsfinallyfiona
finallyfiona.com

5

LIFE AFTER SIDE HUSTLING

At this stage you most probably feel excited and ready for the journey ahead, or maybe you are paralysed with fear because you never planned for this moment. All your feelings are valid and in this chapter we look at practical ways to overcome that fear and press on. Working on your side hustle full time can appear sexy, but I kid you not that running a business is not all fun and games. You have responsibilities – not just personal ones but to your customers, and maybe even investors, if you have those.

MAKING THE TRANSITION

'There's no preparing for this sh*t. Take it a day at a time.'

Some people find themselves in this position not by choice but as a result of circumstance. Maybe you've lost your job, you've gone on maternity leave or you *actually* made the decision to dive in fully. Whatever the reason, how do you transition? I truly believe there is no planning for this and you have to take each day as it comes. I have been in this position twice; the first time was bliss, the second time has been very different. The first time, I was younger and had no responsibilities – planning for a family was years ahead of me and I was free to live as I pleased. The second time, all those responsibilities caught up with me and risk was not looking as sexy as before. Whatever your position, here are a few tips that can help with the transition.

ARE YOU TRULY READY?

Like I mentioned, you may have found yourself in this position because you had no choice but nonetheless are you truly ready to dive in full time or do you need to go back to paid employment? Maybe this is a break for you to explore something new for a short period of time? Have this frank conversation with yourself because it will determine how you show up every day.

Give yourself time to figure it out, but also put your best foot forward for whatever decision you decide. Don't show up half-arsed. If you're going to give this a go, do it damn well.

COMPARISON

You've followed all the entrepreneurs that have inspired you along the journey and now you're in the same position as them, running your side hustle full time. But are you really in the same position? Yes, but they have more experience and have given more time to it, so why are you comparing your chapter with theirs? Don't do it. Continue to see them as inspiration but don't fall into the trap of comparison.

ROUTINE

Your time is yours now; well, it's not really. Get into the habit of creating a routine that will work for you – this may come after a few days of figuring out what the daily tasks will be for you. Routines are the reason why people win at life, that is my opinion. No routine and you'll find yourself confused day in and out.

FINANCE

Maybe you saved for this moment but maybe you didn't. How are you going to financially cope? What are you daily costs? Is your side hustle currently generating enough to fully run itself? Will you need some financial support? Set a budget for what your personal monthly expenses are looking like and how you'll manage it — do the same for your business. I would advise that you do this before the transition but I also know that some of you are not here by choice!

COMMUNITY

I have spoken about this earlier on in the book. Now that things are real, tap into a community of people who are in the same position as you. A community you can fall back on when things get tough. This journey can be lonely, but it doesn't have to be. Lean on people for advice, guidance and support – we are not self-made, so tap into that community.

MINDSET

Go back to the chapter on mindset and get that mind ready for the ups and downs that will surely come. Fill yourself with the wisdom of others, listen to those podcasts, buy those books, take that course and make those notes that will help you stand the test of time.

GET TO WORK

1. Journal how you currently feel about this new position you are in.
2. Journal where you want to be in three months' time. Write it as if you were already there. For example, 'It's three months into running my side hustle full time and I feel fulfilled, supported and financially free.'
3. Create an Excel sheet with the expenses that need to be covered every month for your personal maintenance and also your business. Figure out where you may need to get financial support or cut back on expenses.
4. Who has inspired you this far? Make a list of the women and reach out to them, share your situation, how they have inspired you. What do you want to achieve from reaching out?
5. Create an Excel sheet and jot down how you would like your daily routine to look or do this in a notebook. For example, 8am – wake up and meditate, 9am water plants, 9:30am walk the dog, 11am clean out inbox.

MESSAGE FROM LIZ

You made it this far and I'm glad you've taken the step towards investing in your ideas and betting on yourself. I came up with this book concept in 2018 and it's now 2021; I definitely would have done a few things differently with my own side hustle if I had a simple book like this to help me. But to be honest, so many people have started this journey without a guide, so despite everything I have shared in this book – just start and figure it out as you go along.

Let me know how it is going by reaching out at @elizabethogabi or @forworkingladies. You can also visit www.sidehustleinprogress.com for more resources, and do use the hashtag #SideHustleinProgress

Wishing you success on your journey.

ACKNOWLEDGEMENTS

Many thanks to Omara, my editor, for discovering me and reaching out. Thank you for making my vision a reality.

To my agent, Juliet, thank you for looking out for me.

Thank you to my sisters Temi Conde, Sharla Duncan and Natalie Olarenwaju for always rooting for me and speaking positive words of life into my soul.

A huge shout out to #TeamThirty, led by one of my brilliant mentors, Musa Tariq. Thanks for helping me gain clarity on my purpose, for being great cheerleaders and showing up whenever I need your creativity.

To the magnificent women that are featured in this book and gave me their valuable time, thank you for your words of inspiration.

To the women in the FWL community that inspired this book, thank you for all the support and building this brand with me.

To my mum and dad who now think I am a millionaire because I have a book, thank you for dreaming so big.

A huge thank you to my ever-supporting partner who has been the best emotional support during this process.

Thank God for giving me strength to do this while in a pandemic, my most rewarding experience to date.

RESOURCES

Here is a list of resources that will help you on your side hustle journey, from inspiration to information.

FURTHER READING

PART I: BEFORE THE JOURNEY
The Entrepreneurial Mindset

Invisible Women: Exposing Data Bias in a World Designed for Men, Caroline Criado Perez (Chatto & Windus, 2019)
Mindset: The New Psychology of Success, Carol Dweck (Robinson, 2017)
Grit: Why Passion and Resilience are the Secrets to Success, Angela Duckworth (Vermilion, 2017)
The Fear Fighter Manual, Luvvie Ajayai Jones (Quercus, 2021)
The Magic of Thinking Big, David J. Schwartz (Vermilion, 2016)
Curious: The Desire to Know and Why Your Future Depends on It, Ian Leslie (Quercus, 2015)
Youtube Video: 'A Letter to Fear' by Elizabeth Gilbert

Determining Your Side Hustle

Start With Why, Simon Sinek (Penguin, 2011)
The 4-Hour Work Week, Timothy Ferriss (Vermilion, 2011)

Power Circle

Never Eat Alone, Keith Ferrazzi (Penguin, 2014)
How to Win Friends and Influence People, Dale Carnegie (Vermilion, 2006)

Your Health, the Most Important Asset

Do Less: A Revolutionary Approach to Time and Energy Management for Busy Moms, Kate Northrup (Hay House, 2019)
The Sleep Revolution, Arianna Huffington (Penguin, 2017)
Moody: A Woman's 21st Century Hormone Guide, Amy Thomson (Penguin, 2021)
The Miracle Morning: The 6 Habits That Will Transform Your Life Before 8AM, Hal Elrod (John Murray Learning, 2017)

References

https://pubmed.ncbi.nlm.nih.gov/19934011/
https://pubmed.ncbi.nlm.nih.gov/20053034/

Getting Sh*t Done

Smarter Faster Better: The Secrets of Being Productive in Life and Business, Charles Duhigg (Random House, 2016)
Deep Work: Rules for Focused Success in a Distracted World, Cal Newport (Piatkus, 2016)
ReWork: Change the Way You Work Forever, David Heinemeier Hansson and Jason Fried (Vermilion, 2010)
Atomic Habits, James Clear (Random House Business, 2018)

PART 2: TAKING OFF
How to Get Ideas

The Idea Hunter, Andy Boynton (Jossey-Bass, 2011)
Non-Bullshit Innovation, David Rowan (Bantam Press, 2019)
The Idea in You, Martin Amor and Alex Pellew (Penguin, 2016)

Doing Your Homework

The Mom Test, Rob Fitzpatrick (CreateSpace, 2013)
The Lean Startup, Eric Ries (Portfolio Penguin, 2011)

Experimenting – Building an MVP

The Lean Startup, Eric Ries (Portfolio Penguin, 2011)
Lean B2B: Build Products Businesses Want, Étienne Garbugli (CreateSpace, 2014)

PART 3: BRANDING YOUR IDEA
It's More than Making a Sale

Do Purpose: Why Brands with a Purpose Do Better and Matter More, David Hieatt (The Do Book Company, 2014)
Obsessed: Building a Brand People Love from Day One, Emily Heyward (Portfolio, 2020)

Branding Your Side Hustle

Designing Brand Identity, Alina Wheeler (John Wiley & Sons, 2012)

https://99designs.co.uk/blog
Carl Jung's 12 personality archetypes

Founder as a Brand

Key Person of Influence, Daniel Priestley (Rethink Press, 2014)
I Am My Brand, Kubi Springer (Bloomsbury Business, 2019)
How to Style Your Brand, Fiona Humberstone (Copper Beech Press, 2015)

Getting Your First Customers

Building a StoryBrand, Donald Miller
Contagious, Jonah Berger (Simon Schuster, 2016)
Purple Cow, Seth Godin (Penguin, 2005)
The 22 Immutable Laws of Marketing, Al Ries, Jack Trout (Profile, 1994)

Getting Known

Hype Yourself, Lucy Werner (Practial Inspiration Publishing, 2020)
Show Your Work, Austin Kleon (Workman Publishing, 2014)

Part 4: THE IMPORTANT STUFF
Getting Protected

Do Protect: Legal Advice for Startups, Johnathan Rees (The Do Book Company, 2014)

How Will You Pay for It?

Venture Deals: Be Smarter Than Your Lawyer and Venture Capitalist, Brad Feld and Jason Mendelson (John Wiley & Sons, 2013)
The Crowdsourceress: Get Smart, Get Funded, and Kickstart Your Next Big Idea, Alex Daly (PublicAffairs, 2017)

MORE READING

How to Own the Room, Viv Groskop (Bantam, 2018)
Invisible Women, Caroline Criado-Perez (Chatto & Windus, 2019)
How Will You Measure Your Life, Clayton Christensen (HarperCollins, 2012)
Do Book Series

FURTHER LEARNING AND SUPPORT

LEARNING

Startupschool.org
Sidehustleinprogress.com
Masterclass.com
LinkedIn.com/learning

DIGITAL COMMUNITIES

The-Dots.com
Femstreet.com
Producthunt.com

Elpha.com
Thestack.world

BUSINESS NEWS +

Techcrunch.com
Thingtesting.com
Voguebusiness.com
Sifted.eu
HBR.org
Businessinsider.com
Forcoloredgirlswhotech.substack.com
Courier Media Newsletter

PODCASTS

'How I Made it Happen', with Elizabeth Ogabi
'The Secrets of Wealthy Women', by WSJ
'How I Built This', with Guy Raz
'The Diary of a CEO', with Steven Bartlett
'Techish', with Abadesi Osunsade & Michael Berhane
'Jump Start', by Girlboss Radio
'How to Own the Room', with Vik Groskop
'Confident and Killing It', with Tiwa Ogunlesi

TEAM SUPPORT

Creativemarket.com
Freelancers.com